W9-AVS-056

"John W. Wright presents a new model of preaching that aims to connect the biblical text with congregations in a way that forms them into a true Christian community. Such formation calls for interpretative engagement with both the biblical narrative and the cultural narrative that shape our society. Wright critically surveys current theories of preaching and the variety of hermeneutical practices, providing clear guidance and practical direction for faithful preaching.

Challenging some of the most determinative conceits represented by contemporary American homiletical practices, Wright provides an alternative account of preaching by helping us reclaim a tragic dimension internal to our lives as Christians. Deeply erudite, Wright draws on the work of Hans Frei and George Lindbeck to develop an account of preaching in which the church becomes the subject as well as the agent through which Christians learn again to have their lives narrated by the gospel.

One of the most surprising aspects of this extraordinary book is its ability to help us recognize that current forms of sermon practices can be traced to the Puritan attempt to move the individual from sin to salvation in such a way that it provided reassurance of what it meant to live in God's elect nation. As a result, Wright traces the current accommodated character of American preaching to what people oftentimes associate with a conservative religious movement. This analysis alone makes this an important book, but even more significant, Wright provides a constructive alternative to such accommodated forms of preaching by providing us with examples that can shape an alternative imagination."

STANLEY HAUERWAS, *Gilbert T. Rowe Professor of Theological Ethics, Duke Divinity School*

"Out of his own rich experience as a scholar and preacher, John Wright summons us to 'reinvent' preaching through a rhetoric that draws us out of the comfort zone of a cultural narrative where the biblical text dissolves into a happy ending and, instead, places us into the biblical narrative where we are taken up and transformed by God's story. In clear and compelling language that often rises to eloquence, this book exposes the subtle but almost sinister shift in North American Christianity by which the horizon of contemporary world culture has displaced and replaced the biblical horizon of God's narrative of creation and redemption by a fusion of individual piety and national religion. Authentic preaching then seeks to renarrate a world that makes truth relevant to its own existence by forming a Christian community—the church—that finds its life within God's narrative. Such preaching draws the church out of the world in order to place it back within the world to live out God's narrative of salvation, justice and hope. I wish that I had read this book forty years ago when I began my own preaching ministry!"

RAY S. ANDERSON, *Senior Professor of Theology and Ministry, Fuller Theological Seminary*

"John Wright very clearly exposes both the prevalence and dangers of the split between 'personal salvation' and 'mission of the nation-state' preaching in North American culture and calls us instead to the kind of preaching that will immerse our listeners in God's larger story. His many helpful insights into such topics as a 'homiletic of turning,' comedic versus tragic moves, therapeutic and managerial functions, and elements of congregational contexts will positively affect your preaching and pastoral care. This is a significantly constructive book!"

DR. MARVA J. DAWN, *theologian, author, educator with Christians Equipped for Ministry, and Teaching Fellow in Spiritual Theology at Regent College, Vancouver, British Columbia*

"If you think preaching should focus on getting individuals to heaven and guiding America (back) to greatness, then do not read this book. If you think that Christians make the church and that its purpose is to help them, then run away from this book. For here John Wright proclaims the biblical gospel that God intends the church 'as the visible body of Christ in the world.' Setting the biblical story over against cultural stories that have falsified the gospel and emaciated preaching, Wright calls for a homiletic reformation that preaches the congregation into the biblical story. Wright is right about what is wrong with our preaching and our churches, and his corrective guidance in this book is the cure we need. Attentive to rhetoric, filled with pastoral insight and sermonic exemplifications, this book is essential assistance in becoming 'the rhetorical embodiment of the biblical story'—that is, the church."

BRENT LAYTHAM, *Associate Professor of Theology and Ethics, North Park Theological Seminary*

"The church should be worried about this book. It comes as an invitation to rethink the task of preaching, but three pages into it you'll realize that Wright is not giving us another 'how-to' book for adding to the plethora of 'messages' delivered every Sunday. No, this little book is packed with minor-prophet-like punch, arguing that preaching is the practice by which the North American church has fallen, but also giving us a glimpse of how preaching could help it stand. Providing a brilliant historical and theological diagnosis of the problem with so-called biblically based, need-centered preaching (whether liberal or conservative), *Telling God's Story* winsomely sketches what authentic 'biblical' preaching looks like: not conscripting the Bible to legitimate the cultural narratives of consumerist individualism or triumphant nationalism, but rather finding ourselves in the biblical story as an alternative to both. If the church is properly said to be a *polis*, then this book unpacks the 'politics' of homiletics. It should be required reading in seminaries across North America. And we could hope that pastors already immersed in ministry would be willing to risk reading this book. But be forewarned: it will radically change your understanding of your charge to 'preach the gospel.'"

JAMES K. A. SMITH, *Associate Professor of Philosophy, Calvin College*

"This is an important and timely book. John Wright has presented us with an excellent volume on narrative preaching. As you would expect of a good text on preaching, it is very helpful with regard to the mechanics of narrative preaching. But Dr. Wright offers us much more, especially as he embeds narrative preaching in a thoughtful and reflective ecclesiology. The book is written in such a way that the reader experiences what the book describes as Dr. Wright leads us through discussions of preaching as comedy and tragedy and ultimately through narrative preaching as a means of inviting listeners to participate in the redemptive story of God. This volume will be an invaluable resource to both preachers and students of preaching."

RON BENEFIEL, *President, Nazarene Theological Seminary*

TELLING GOD'S STORY

Narrative Preaching for Christian Formation

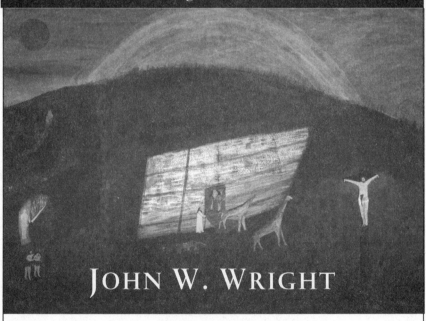

JOHN W. WRIGHT

IVP Academic

An imprint of InterVarsity Press
Downers Grove, Illinois

InterVarsity Press
P.O. Box 1400, Downers Grove, IL 60515-1426
World Wide Web: www.ivpress.com
E-mail: email@ivpress.com

InterVarsity Press® is the book-publishing division of InterVarsity Christian Fellowship/USA®, a student movement active on campus at hundreds of universities, colleges and schools of nursing in the United States of America, and a member movement of the International Fellowship of Evangelical Students. For information about local and regional activities, write Public Relations Dept., InterVarsity Christian Fellowship/USA, 6400 Schroeder Rd., P.O. Box 7895, Madison, WI 53707-7895, or visit the IVCF website at <www.intervarsity.org>.

Design: Cindy Kiple
Images: Ricco/Maresca Gallery/Art Resource, NY

ISBN 978-0-8308-2740-4

Printed in the United States of America ∞

Library of Congress Cataloging-in-Publication Data

Wright, John W., 1959-
  Telling God's story: narrative preaching for Christian formation /
John W. Wright.
    p. cm
  Includes bibliographical references.
  ISBN 978-0-8308-2740-4 (pbk.: alk. paper)
  1. Narrative preaching. 2. Preaching. 3. Bible—Hermeneutics. I.
Title.
BV4235.S76W75 2007
251—dc22

                                                                 2007004007

| **P** | 19 | 18 | 17 | 16 | 15 | 14 | 13 | 12 | 11 | 10 | 9 | 8 | 7 | 6 | 5 | 4 | 3 | 2 | 1 |
| **Y** | 23 | 22 | 21 | 20 | 19 | 18 | 17 | 16 | 15 | 14 | 13 | 12 | 11 | 10 | 09 | 08 | 07 |

CONTENTS

ACKNOWLEDGMENTS

This book was conceived as a two-year project that has come to full gestation after over a decade. I have many to thank for their support and contributions that helped see this book to completion. Reverend Dr. Stephen Green was instrumental in forming the preaching ideas found here. Through a jointly authored paper, given in 1997 at the Association of Nazarene Sociologists of Religion in Kansas City, Missouri, Reverend Dr. Ron Benefiel helped work out a portion of chapter two. Rodney Clapp, then an editor at IVP, initially encouraged the project; his successor, Dr. Gary Deddo, and his IVP staff, have sustained the project across time and contributed their considerable expertise and graciousness to its successful completion. Colleagues at Point Loma Nazarene University, Dr. Karl Martin and Reverend Dr. Robert Smith, read all or parts of the manuscript. Their encouragement and friendship have been invaluable to me. Reverend Jason and Maya Evoy and Reverend Dr. Darrel Poeppelmeyer read the manuscript in its early stages and offered valuable insight for its revision. The anonymous reviewer provided by IVP also gave excellent, truthful suggestions to an earlier draft, which helped clarify my thought and writing. God has also surrounded me with a multitude of friends, for whom I give thanks.

The book is also a product of the life that I live, which is deeply embedded in three related but distinct institutions that compose my life: the church, the academy and my family. Two congregations—First Church of the Nazarene in Winamac, Indiana, and the Church of the Nazarene in Mid-City, San Diego (English-speaking congregation)—have provided the grist of pastoral experience that is infused throughout the book. Point Loma Nazarene University has supported the project through a

Wesley Fellowship from the Wesleyan Center for Twenty-First Century Studies, a RASP grant to allow travel in its early stages, a sabbatical during which I completed the bulk of the manuscript and a myriad of the most wonderful students that one could ever imagine. They help me to remember why I do what I do.

The project would not have reached completion without the profound gift of my family, Reverend Kathy Wright and my four children, Johnny, Carl, Tony and Tasha. We have been through much together since this book was conceived. We moved from the rural Midwest to "sunny Southern California." Once here, "Dad" has spent much of his time moving constantly between church and university as a bivocational professor/pastor/scholar. As a family, we have stood together as we planted an urban congregation with people from all over the globe, encountered the nitty-gritty of the life of the church among the poor, consistently enfolded other children into the household, worked through the stresses and strains of congregational life, and spent hours on the sidelines and in the game during the perpetual soccer season that life is. I cannot express the depth of gratitude to God for my family—for their stability, love and support of me during this time.

INTRODUCTION

This book arose out of personal experience. I had finished my Ph.D. in theology at the University of Notre Dame. I had spent years studying to become a Scripture scholar. I had enjoyed the honor of studying the Scriptures with some of the best biblical scholars in the world. After several years as a visiting professor, I was called to pastor in Winamac, Indiana. Winamac is a small town of 2,300 in rural Indiana, a town, as I like to describe it, "sixty miles away from the nearest mall." Winamac is the county seat of Pulaski County. Agriculture still reigns in Pulaski County. Deer were so plentiful that they were seen as vermin. The county records more car accidents involving deer than accidents involving other cars.

The pastorate was a profound experience for me. I learned much. I learned how to load hogs to take them to market, how to climb into a duck blind before dawn in subfreezing weather. I even got to drive a combine to harvest beans. I'm sure Bill Tetzloff is still laughing at the wheelie that I managed to pop with the combine as I learned how to control the hand levers. I entered the pastorate completely, joyously and thankfully.

The problem was preaching. My biblical and theological studies, as well as my life, had convinced me of the importance of the church to live as a "contrast society" or an "alternative community" amid North American society. I was persuaded—and still am—that in the life, death and resurrection of Jesus and the gift of the Holy Spirit, God had begun a new age of God's peaceable kingdom and called both Jew and Gentile, male and female, slave and free to live together as a witness to God's rule that will ultimately extend through all creation in the coming of

Christ. At the most fundamental level I believed—and still do—that this conviction sets an entirely different agenda for Christians. The particular practices and convictions of the church, not the practices of the market-driven North American society, must determine the formation, the witness and the ministry of the church. To convey the difference between the *church* and *world* by calling people into an alternative set of practices through preaching, I discovered, was a very difficult task. We had all learned that "church" really existed to help individuals deal with their own personal struggles.

It was not connecting to the local culture that made preaching difficult for me. I had deep roots in rural Midwestern life. Nor was the task difficult because North American society had passed into a postmodern or post-Christian era—Winamac hadn't yet. The nativity scene still made its appearance on the courthouse lawn. Most everyone in town was convinced that the church and good, respectable American morals were one and the same.

I discovered that the presuppositions of Christendom were a major part of the problem. It was very difficult to maintain a Christological focus for the life of the believer and the church. In a certain sense, each person or family perceived themselves at the center of the life of the church. The congregation was deeply convinced that God's love shown in Jesus by the power of the Holy Spirit was really about "me" and the fulfillment of "my personal needs."

My homiletical training was largely in deductive, exegetical preaching. My congregation, however, had experienced years of a different type of homiletical formation, one based in various contemporary versions of the revivalist tradition. Within this tradition the church gathers to enable individuals to find God's help for various personal problems. Instead of preaching to feed them as individuals, I attempted to proclaim the wonderful good news that God had called them together as a peculiar people to live as a kingdom of priests, a holy nation for the sake of the nations. The wonders of God's grace included folk in such out-of-the-way places as first-century Galilee and late twentieth-century Winamac.

I met a confusing problem, however. Only a small minority could hear my preaching, largely those among the senior saints of the church. For much of the congregation, especially baby boomers, I was met with a polite blankness or even open antagonism. I was not preaching to meet their needs. More frustrating, I did not have the homiletical skills necessary for the majority of the congregation to discover the real issue that the biblical narrative raises for their lives.

Thankfully, a friend referred me to a pastor of a large church on the West Coast, Dr. Stephen Green. I had heard of Steve, but I had never met or talked with him. In desperation I called him early one Monday afternoon. Despite his busy life and many responsibilities, Steve graciously took my call and immediately provided three things for me. First, he referred me to the homiletical work of David Buttrick. Second, we found a deep theological friendship. Third, Steve agreed to send me tapes of his sermons as he preached them.

I ordered David Buttrick's *Homiletic* and read it immediately. Buttrick's work gave me a rhetorical structure that allowed the congregation to follow the progression of my sermon. I had little sympathy, however, with the liberal theological commitments underpinning Buttrick's work. More importantly, Steve's sermons opened up a completely new homiletical vista for me. I could hear Buttrick's forms and structures in Steve's sermons, but the theological agenda was very different. Steve sought to redirect his congregation into the biblical narrative from the narratives that their North American society had provided them. We discussed the precise rhetoric that Steve employed, and I began experimenting with a similar rhetoric in my preaching. No longer did my sermons shoot over the head of my congregation. Steve had given me a way of connecting with my congregation and moving them into the biblical text.

Our conversation continued. I moved to Point Loma Nazarene University in San Diego, California, not far from where Steve pastored. We decided to pursue a book together in order to cast the homiletical rhetoric that Steve had developed into a broader hermeneutical, historical and ecclesial context. Steve, however, soon moved to a new assignment, combining college teaching with the pastorate of a large congregation. The task of writing fell to me. This book is the result.

Much of this work and its central homiletical insight belong to Steve, though I am responsible for its precise articulation in this text. I am extremely thankful for the perspective Steve has provided, both for this book and in my preaching and teaching. I contemplated using the first-person plural "we" throughout the book as a reminder to myself and to the reader of Steve's involvement in the project. However, my editor talked me out of it.

The goal of this book is to present a specific homiletical rhetoric that may shape congregations into distinctive, alternative Christian communities. In other words, I seek to explore how to preach in order to form a congregation into a "peculiar people."[1] To accomplish this end, the book ranges far and wide. I begin with a contemporary review of theories of interpretation in order to argue that preaching is not merely a technique of application subsequent to interpretation. I believe that at the very core of its practice, preaching represents interpretation par excellence. This awareness allows the preacher to embrace an aspect of preaching usually shunned—what is called the "tragic moment" in interpretation.

The book then moves to a historical, cultural and theological analysis of the narrative horizons of much of North American Christianity. This analysis allows us to explore detrimental theological tendencies in North American Christianity from within, narratives that compete with the biblical story for the formation of Christian life and convictions. By denaturalizing these stories, a way is opened to see differently, to move out of these narratives into the story of God as narrated in the Christian Scriptures.

Chapter three represents the central chapter in the book. Here the biblical narrative is summarized as the context for presenting a specific homiletic rhetoric, a homiletic of turning. The concept of homiletical moves opens a way to shift a congregation from narratives provided by the general North American culture into living within the biblical narrative. Rather than translating the biblical text into relevant categories for lives shaped by a fallen and sinful world, the chapter puts forth a concrete rhetoric to form a congregation into a people who find their lives, collectively and individually, as characters within the biblical story. Chapter four provides specific sermonic illustrations with accompanying theological and homiletical commentary.

Chapter five places a homiletic of turning into a broader pastoral the-

---

[1]The reference is to Rodney Clapp's book, *A Peculiar People: The Church as Culture in a Post-Christian Society* (Downers Grove, Ill.: InterVarsity Press, 1996).

ology and practice. Rather than forming a church adept at becoming assimilated to its surrounding culture, the chapter encourages movement beyond the therapeutic pastorate in order to embrace embodiment of the biblical narrative for the sake of the distinctive witness of the church. The chapter recommends particular, concrete congregational practices that render the biblical story intelligible to the congregation and to the world. These practices themselves provide a rhetorical context for preaching. Such a context empowers the hearing of the tragic moment in interpretation as the condition for living life within God's story as narrated by the Christian Scriptures.

I hope that this book finds an audience in young students and ministers just starting their way into God's call in the service of the church. I also hope to provide a guide for pastoral preaching and care for the concrete adventure of leading God's people into faithful witness and evangelism in the world. The book seeks to address conscientious, experienced pastors who care deeply about the Christian formation of those God has entrusted to their pastoral care. The book hopefully conveys the respect for those who undertake such a task, fully cognizant of its difficulty.

Yet I also look to reform pastoral preaching and care from those often given in contemporary models and practice. There is a movement within this book itself (not separate from homiletical rhetoric that it presents). The book embraces a tragic moment, even in the ministry of its reader. This is in no way to cast aspersions on the sacrificial ministry of pastors, nor to deny God's use of such means for God's glory. Yet I bring to light deeply held narrative convictions and contrast them with the biblical vision, so that the pastoral and ecclesial witness might shine forth ever more clearly in the world with a missional integrity. If God will form the church into a peculiar people in North America, God will use the faithful ministry of pastors who have found themselves living within the biblical narrative for the glory of God. The formation of such a church will not take place in learned academic halls but in the daily lives of concrete congregations who will courageously embody the biblical text in the practices that form their lives and witness in the world.

God has graced my life as a pastor with the Winamac Church of the Nazarene in Winamac, Indiana, and now in the Church of the Nazarene in Mid-City, San Diego. Amid the saints that God has gathered and continues to gather in these places, this book is dedicated to the memory of Sue Link.

I'll never forget the morning after a sermon when Sue looked up at me after discovering that the story of the Scripture was not directly about her but God—and therefore about her. The Spirit worked mightily in Sue, forming her into a beautiful witness to all who came into contact with her, including myself, my wife, Kathy, and my four children, especially Carl, my middle child. Several years after we left Winamac, Sue was tragically killed in a head-on collision on a country road not far from her home. Earlier that Sunday morning, Sue had collected pictures and notes from the children of the congregation. She was going to take them to a hospital one hundred miles away in Indianapolis where the mother of several of the children lay, dying of cancer. It was just one of the little ways that Sue constantly cared for the needs of the saints and showed hospitality to strangers. Sue's character identified her as a follower of Jesus Christ. She most definitely was a "peculiar person" in the best sense of the phrase.

If God can use preaching to form the church as a contrast society to form people like Sue Link, and if this book can contribute in any way to this end, I will be very thankful. It is in the character of such saints as Sue that the truthfulness, integrity and credibility of God's story, the Scriptural narrative from Genesis through Revelation, will shine forth so that the world might see, and in seeing, believe.

1

HOMILETICS AS
BIBLICAL HERMENEUTICS

Those who concentrate on trying to discover the "real meaning" of the text overlook the fact that the church is charged week after week to practice preaching. It is not as if preaching explicates the same invariant meaning of the text, applying it to different circumstances, but rather that preaching helps us see that what is at stake is not the question of "the meaning of Scripture" but the usefulness of Scripture, given the good ends of Christian community. The Scriptures are exhibited in communities that are capable of pointing to holy lives through which we can rightly see the reality that has made the Scriptures possible.[1]

Preaching is an odd practice within the contemporary world. We live in an age of spin doctors, three-second sound bites and a continuous barrage of visual images. Prolonged discourse spoken in constant reference to an ancient text seems curiously outmoded. Preaching seems to exist as a nostalgic nod of the church to a tradition shaped from a world as far away as Mars.

Of course, the contemporary oddness of preaching isn't news to most preachers. The past twenty-five years have seen far-reaching shifts in the presentation of the sermon. Pulpits have disappeared. Those remaining are often small, narrow or even clear podiums on a auditorium-like stage. Taking a clue from motivational speakers and empowered by wireless microphones, clergy have learned mobility in a desperate attempt to engage people formed by the constant visual stream of televi-

---

[1]Stanley Hauerwas, *Unleashing the Scripture: Freeing the Bible from Captivity in America* (Nashville: Abingdon, 1993), p. 37.

sion. Even the word *preaching* has dropped out of fashion. Preaching represents an undesirable vestige of stuffy churchiness. Preachers no longer preach or proclaim the gospel. Instead, they share or, better, engage in a teaching ministry. Printed outlines with fill-in-the-blanks ensure that those who gather follow the message and take helpful tips home. Congregations demand relevance, insight into life as lived by the mainstream of North American culture. Preachers constantly face the specter of two unpardonable sins, sins beyond the realm of atonement: not meeting the people's needs and, even worse, boring them. Preaching has become a perilous activity.

In the academy, preaching has not fared much better. Despite a recent disciplinary resurgence, homiletics, the study of preaching, seems far removed from the intellectually rigorous realms of academic biblical interpretation, church history and theology. Academics tend to regard preaching as at least one step removed from the authentic interpretation of the biblical text. From the perspective of the academy, preaching remains subordinate to the specialized scholar's interpretive practices. Only trained specialists have the expertise to determine the meaning of a biblical text; preachers artfully supply the rhetorical packaging of the specialist's previous work.

Theological education commonly reflects such priorities. Seminaries regularly demand multiple levels of exegetical classes. The student begins with introduction to Old Testament and New Testament classes—classes often unrelated to each other. A class in hermeneutics, or the theory of interpretation, often follows to take students through principled methodological steps in interpretation. As a student heads toward graduation, upper division classes on specific biblical books or theological issues appear on the curricular menu. Finally, the curriculum reserves preaching for one, maybe two, classes at the end of the student's seminary career. Preaching classes apply what the student has mastered in their scientific study of the biblical books in the hypothetical historical context of their composition.

Once called to a congregation, however, preachers face radically changed priorities. The conscientious preacher may still do extensive exegetical homework to prepare for the sermon. Yet relevance to the life of a local congregation always looms large in the formation of the sermon. Of course, not all preachers have the luxury of being conscientious. Pastoral, administrative and personal pressures quickly fill each day with exhausting demands. Yet the weekly task of the sermon still remains.

But that is not all. Each sermon must fulfill the expectations of the congregation—expectations usually formed by the consumerist, entertainment-oriented society we live in. Clergy have instinctively responded to the situation. The difference between the interests of the academy to determine the text's historical meaning and a congregation's concern for relevance is obvious. Preachers face extraordinary pressure to abandon academic readings of the Scriptures for contemporary relevance. After all, professional biblical scholars do not attend many board meetings. The serious engagement of the biblical text itself becomes shaped by accommodation to the contemporary world. The concern for daily living can easily overwhelm the voice of the biblical text, except in the faint echo of biblical citations.

Such dynamics often lead to even more academic denigration of preaching or preachers. Biblical scholars and professional theologians commonly bemoan the abandonment or distortion of biblical texts within contemporary preaching. From the preacher's perspective, however, there is another side to the story. For preachers, it is apparent that the academy, even the theological academy, has abandoned the church. Academic biblical exegesis is at best practiced only indirectly within any ecclesial context. Within the academy, promotion and tenure come with the publication of books and articles in scholarly journals, not with the oral presentation of sermons. When preachers turn to the work of biblical scholars, they sense a different concern at work, the concern of the professional guild in service of the scholar's career advancement. Given the contemporary oddity of preaching and the time constraints placed on the clergy, preachers have little time or tolerance to wade through detailed academic discussions that at best bear indirectly on the concerns that the congregants bring into their gathering.

The split between academic biblical exegesis and preaching reflects a divide drawn by contemporary North American culture. Robert Bellah has described these realms as the "managerial" and the "therapeutic" realms.[2] American culture strongly differentiates between these two realms. Professional biblical scholarship exists within and for the managerial realm. Here the biblical text is read for its objective, public, abstract, rational, historical and principled meaning. Academic readings are offered to the academic guild to contribute to the well-ordered functioning of the society. Preaching, however, is practiced within and for the subjective, private, concrete, therapeutic realm of the individual. Preaching is to help people adjust to the often cruel demands of the managerial realm, to help compensate for the disorder wrought in individual lives from conforming to the competitive, impersonal order of the managerial realm. If these are the only two options, if a preacher must pick between the two realms of the managerial and therapeutic, congregational expectations will guide the sermon into the therapeutic realm every time. Repeating a recent popular mantra, in such a therapeutic context, preaching must become need-centered and biblically based.

Yet other options exist. The bifurcation between biblical interpretation and preaching is an extremely recent phenomenon in the life of the church. We only need to thumb through sermons before the modern era to understand the role of homiletics as the central practice for the biblical formation of believers throughout Christian history. For instance, the homilies of Origen often were given to new believers preparing for baptism. John Wesley's "Standard Sermons" functioned as the doctrinal standards of his early Methodist Societies, and even the sermons of Paul Tillich far outsold his *Systematic Theology*.[3] The long trajectory of Christian proclamation stands in sharp contrast to the contemporary situation.

---

[2]Robert Bellah et al., *Habits of the Heart: Individualism and Commitment in American Life* (Berkeley: University of California Press, 1996), pp. 44-48; Dorothy Smith describes the same cultural bifurcation from a feminist perspective as the difference between the "extralocal" and the "local" (see *The Everyday World as Problematic: A Feminist Sociology* [Boston: Northeastern University Press, 1987]).

[3]"It was not only Tillich's volumes of systematic theology, but also his sermons, particularly those in *The Shaking of Foundations*, that were influential. For example, in *Honest to God*, . . . John A. T. Robinson drew heavily from the work of Tillich. However, what is easily overlooked is the fact that Robinson frequently cites not Tillich's *Systematic Theology*, but his sermons. In addition, Tillich's theology and preaching exercised an important influence during the early stages of the development of narrative homiletics" (Charles Campbell, *Preaching Jesus: New Directions for Homiletics in Hans Frei's Postliberal Theology* [Grand Rapids: Eerdmans, 1997], p. 41).

The present situation cannot be beneficial for the church. Preaching has largely ceased to incorporate individuals into the concerns created by the Christian Scriptures. Instead, preaching has become the application of an individualistic, therapeutic biblical language to contemporary concerns or disembodied calls to social justice.

The church in North America has become adept at translating the Scriptures into the narratives that already shape the lives of believers and nonbelievers alike. By providing a private, therapeutic, individualistic biblical discourse, such preaching maintains the presence of the church as a voluntary grouping of individuals living in a society that looks to the church for personal fulfillment rather than public guidance. Recent developments in inductive and narrative homiletics support the therapeutic role of preaching. As Charles Campbell astutely observes:

> Although narrative homiletics takes a variety of forms, at the center of the major works in the area is an emphasis on human experience. . . . Unlike older cognitive models, narrative preaching seeks to touch the hearer at the "level of experience." . . . Narrative is valued for its distinctive ability to produce or evoke experience.[4]

The biblical text becomes translated into a therapeutic experience within the life of the individual. Yet it seems that such an approach misses the crucial question, a question necessary to maintain the faithful witness of the church across time. The question is not, How can we make the Scriptures relevant to individuals in need of therapy? but, How do we translate human lives into the biblical narrative to live as part of the body of Christ in the world?

This latter question guides this book: How might preachers develop a homiletical rhetoric that provides for the Scriptural formation of the church as a peculiar people, a kingdom of priests, a holy nation? I believe that a nostalgic return to an idyllic age long past is neither possible nor desirable. Would we really like a return to Puritan New England where two-hour Sunday sermons governed church and society by the force of ecclesial authority, or revivalist preaching that inspires personal guilt with life-long psychological scarring? I think not. Nor will merely reacting do; preachers cannot act like ostriches, burying their head in the

---

[4]Ibid., p. 122.

sand while the world passes by. We must address the contemporary realities constructively. Whenever a preacher looks out to a congregation, these realities stare back at him or her. Preaching is a rhetorical practice. A new rhetorical situation demands new tactics for preaching.

Yet rhetoric alone will not completely address the contemporary situation. Our first challenge is to understand and heal the chasm between interpretation and preaching, a distinction that plays itself out as the chasm between the academy and the church. More technically, we must understand interpretation is not prior to homiletics; homiletics already *is* interpretation. We will discover that contemporary interpretative theory, or hermeneutics, suggests that the distinction between interpretation and application has been far overdrawn in our contemporary understanding. At its most profound level homiletics reveals dynamics that occur in all interpretation, biblical or otherwise. Homiletics is not the poor country cousin of academic biblical interpretation. Homiletics is professional biblical scholarship's older sibling, opening the biblical text to its hearers afresh and anew. Homiletics chiefly differs from the academic and historical reading of biblical texts in the openness and honesty by which it approaches its task.

My ultimate purpose, however, is not to use homiletics in order to review contemporary interpretative theory. My purpose is pastoral and, therefore, theological. Understanding homiletics as illustrative of hermeneutics reveals possibilities latent within preaching. These possibilities have always been inherent in preaching. Nonetheless, they have usually been undeveloped in theory and in practice. Approaching homiletics through contemporary hermeneutics may open up the biblical text for a new, more powerful hearing.

My ultimate goal is to establish a homiletical rhetoric that can aid the formation of the church as an alternative people, a people united to each other in Christ beyond socioeconomic, national, ethnic and gender roles provided by powerful forces of formation in the world today. This is no easy task. The contemporary North American culture emits amazing powers to assimilate groups to its own ends in the name of pluralism. Yet through a hermeneutical and historical analysis, I will explore opening up a new space through preaching whereby the Word of God might call forth a people able to live faithful to the God of Israel, the God of Jesus Christ.

Homiletics, Hermeneutics and Reflections on the Hermeneutical Event

Preaching has not always been a secondary location for biblical interpretation. Christian biblical interpretation began in the context of the pastoral care of Christian lives. Only in the past several centuries has homiletics been forced to the margins of biblical interpretation. A brief trip through modern intellectual history may help us understand how this situation developed. More recent developments, however, have provided the possibility of retrieving preaching as the primary location for the interpretation of the Christian Scriptures. These developments might at first sound very strange, even threatening, to preachers trained in the rigors of historico-grammatical interpretation. Such a reading seems to honor the biblical text because it provides a specific method in order to isolate the real historical meaning of the Bible.[5] Yet the price of this honor turns the Scriptures into a relic. Recent hermeneutical theory has actually returned interpretation much closer to the early Christian theory that guided the church in the premodern era.[6]

Three figures stand out in the intellectual history that forms the backdrop to this story: Friedrich Schleiermacher, Martin Heidegger and Hans-Georg Gadamer. A fourth, Jacque Derrida, looms in the shadows. Martin Heidegger's *Being and Time,* published first in 1927, forms the pivotal text in our story. Heidegger placed interpretation at the center of philosophical discourse. Today, whether one talks about structures of scientific revolutions, feminist theory, symbolic social systems or reading acquisition in children, hermeneutics plays a fundamental role in the discussion. Yet to understand the precise interplay between homiletics and hermeneutics, it is best to begin before Heidegger—with the prominent nineteenth century theologian and preacher, Friedrich Schleiermacher.

In the early nineteenth century Friedrich Schleiermacher transformed hermeneutics into a universal discipline for interpreting all lan-

---

[5]For an older generation see A. Berkeley Mickelsen, *Interpreting the Bible* (Grand Rapids: Eerdmans, 1963). For a more recent exemplar, see Gordon D. Fee and Douglas Stuart, *How to Read the Bible for All Its Worth,* 3rd ed. (Grand Rapids: Zondervan, 2003).

[6]See, i.e., Gerald L. Bruns, *Hermeneutics Ancient and Modern* (New Haven, Conn.: Yale University Press, 1992); and Jean Grondin, *Introduction to Philosophical Hermeneutics,* Yale Studies in Hermeneutics (New Haven, Conn.: Yale University Press, 1994).

guage.[7] Schleiermacher desired to drive ambiguity completely out of interpretation. By grounding special cases of interpretation in a more general art, Schleiermacher thought that hermeneutics could provide a rigorous universal method to understand the meaning of any language objectively. Arbitrariness in the interpretation of any language grew "out of the chaotic conditions of the discipline" and will not dissipate "until hermeneutics assumes the technical form it is due."[8] The theorist, for Schleiermacher, must develop systematic, self-contained rules that could move interpretation toward universally certain, scientific results.[9] Schleiermacher expanded hermeneutics to a universal discipline in order to achieve tighter control over interpretation through applying methodological rules.

Schleiermacher's broadening of hermeneutics directly relates to his understanding of the aim of interpretation. Hermeneutics, for Schleiermacher, forms universal interpretive rules so that one may interpret correctly. Schleiermacher's negative statement of the goal of hermeneutics has received most attention: the task of hermeneutics is "to avoid qualitative and quantitative misunderstandings."[10] Yet Schleiermacher also recognized that a negative definition alone was inadequate—a negative formulation does not allow the development of clear, definitive rules. A positive formulation of the task of hermeneutics is necessary to develop such rules.[11] Schleiermacher perhaps de-

---

[7] "To orient hermeneutics to understanding has proved to be Schleiermacher's lasting contribution to the history of hermeneutical theory. By virtue of this achievement he can lay claim to the title of 'founder' of modern hermeneutics" (James Duke, "Translators' Introduction," in Friedrich Schleiermacher, *Hermeneutics: The Unpublished Manuscripts,* ed. Heinz Kimmerle, American Academy of Religion Texts and Translation Series 1 [Atlanta: Scholars Press, 1986], p. 15).

[8] Friedrich Schleiermacher, *Hermeneutics: The Unpublished Manuscripts,* ed. Heinz Kimmerle, American Academy of Religion Texts and Translation Series 1 (Atlanta: Scholars Press, 1986), p. 214.

[9] "In general a special hermeneutics is only an abbreviated procedure which must be governed by general rules. But when the special hermeneutics degenerates into a collection of observations, then this abbreviation has been made at the expense of the scientific character and so, too, of its certainty" (ibid., p. 122).

[10] Ibid., p.70.

[11] "This thesis (17) encompasses the full task of interpretation, but because it is stated negatively we cannot develop rules from it. In order to develop rules we must work from a positive thesis, but we must constantly be oriented to this negative formulation" (ibid., p. 111).

fined most clearly the positive task of hermeneutics in his *Outline:* "The goal of all interpretation consists in correctly apprehending each individual thought in its relationship to the idea of the whole and, in doing this, likewise in reconstructing the act of writing."[12] Similarly, within his lectures, Schleiermacher wrote, "The task [of hermeneutics] is to be formulated as follows: 'To understand the text at first as well and then even better than its author.'"[13]

Perhaps Schleiermacher's position now seems commonsensical rather than innovative. Many today presuppose that interpretation is about the re-presentation of the author's meaning in the interpreter's consciousness. Through the disciplined use of universal rules, preachers have been taught that they may recover the singular meaning of the text as the author intended. Hermeneutics is an historical, repetitive, excavational discipline, the artful inverse of language production.[14]

Schleiermacher's two realms of interpretation, the grammatical and the technical, are the mirror image of a speaker's/author's production of speech/text: "Just as the first side [grammatical interpretation] is the reverse of grammar, so the second side [technical interpretation] is the reverse side of composition."[15] By methodologically and artfully retracing the path of the production of speech or a text, one ultimately may avoid misunderstanding and thus understand a text as well as, if not better than, the author.

The consequences of Schleiermacher's position for preaching are far-reaching. Schleiermacher's general hermeneutics made interpretation a strictly historical task. He drove a wedge deeply between interpretation and explication, between understanding and application, or as popularized by Krister Stendahl, between what a text meant and what it means.[16] Schleiermacher consistently upheld this distinction throughout all his lectures on hermeneutics, from his very first point in 1809 to his final

---

[12]Friedrich Schleiermacher, *Brief Outline of Theology as a Field of Study: Translation of the 1822 and 1830 Editions,* ed. and trans. Terrence N. Tice, Schleiermacher Studies and Translations 1 (Lewiston: Edwin Mellen, 1990), p. 72 n. 79.

[13]Schleiermacher, *Hermeneutics,* p. 112.

[14]"Every act of understanding is the reverse side of an act of speaking, and one must grasp the thinking that underlies a given statement" (ibid., p. 97).

[15]Ibid., p. 62.

[16]See Krister Stendahl, *Meanings: The Bible as Document and Guide* (Philadelphia: Fortress, 1984).

lecture in 1830.[17] Quite simply, for Schleiermacher, "Hermeneutics deals only with the art of understanding, not with the presentation of what has been understood."[18] His quest for a universal discipline of hermeneutics removes the text effectively from the interpreter's contemporary world. The "meaning" of the text becomes confined to the past. Schleiermacher's hermeneutic provided a powerful apology for historico-grammatical and historical-critical readings as the sole legitimate interpretation of the biblical text.

Of course, such an understanding severely separates preaching from biblical interpretation. Before one can preach, one must first act as an historian. From Schleiermacher's perspective, preaching can even endanger truthful interpretation. Homiletics can interfere with biblical interpretation by bringing contemporary concerns to the text prematurely. The preacher must strongly differentiate between interpretation and application. For Schleiermacher and the legion of his heirs, hermeneutics is about obtaining meaning; homiletics about the application of the text to a specific, concrete situation. Hermeneutics is about historical retrieval; homiletics about contemporary significance. Homiletics *depends on* hermeneutics—and the technical academic scholar—that determines *the* meaning of the biblical text. The preacher must then encase this meaning into an appropriate rhetorical shell for its homiletical presentation to a congregation.

Relegated to the realm of historians, biblical interpretation becomes separated from the use of the Scriptures within and for the life of the church. Modern preaching is left to develop under the watchful, regulative eye of the professional exegete/historian. Leaving the interpretive work to others, or at least separating it before one begins the homiletical task, the preacher is to find an appropriate application for the biblical text once the specialist has excavated the text's singular meaning. This

---

[17]1809: "Only what Ermesti (Prol., sec. 4) calls *subtilitas intelligendi* (exactness of understanding) genuinely belongs to hermeneutics. As soon as the *subtilitas explicandi* (exactness of application) becomes more than the outer side of understanding, it becomes part of the art of presentation, and is itself subject to hermeneutics" (Schleiermacher, *Hermeneutics*, p. 41). 1830: "If the interpreter does this deliberately, he is no longer engaged in interpretation but in practical application; if he does it unintentionally, his explanation is simply false" (ibid., p. 213).

[18]Ibid., p. 97.

is the reason that preachers have always struggled with the historical-critical method: it denies the direct contemporaneity of the Scriptures that preaching from the Scriptures presupposes—that God has sanctified this particular text to reveal God's own triune Self in the present.[19] In contrast, for Schleiermacher, Scripture speaks only through the mediation of the human author of the text. We can interpret the Scriptures only in so far as we remove ourself from our own concrete body, transposing ourself into the mind of the author, now dead.

Such an understanding suggests that the Scripture no longer directly addresses a congregation. Schleiermacher's theory of interpretation contests the very practice of reading Scriptures as the Word of God to a contemporary congregation. Preaching presupposes that the Scriptures are not only an archive of the Word of God to the church in the past; the Scriptures are the Word of God to the church today—directly and immediately by the power of the Spirit of the triune God who is the final Author of the Scriptures. Schleiermacher's understanding of interpretation places preachers in a quandary by divorcing the discovery of the text's meaning in the past from its application in the present. The preacher must first address one audience in preparation for the sermon—the objective, abstract, rational, disembodied human being—to find *the* meaning of the text and then move to a second audience, the very particular, located, concrete life of a congregation and individuals within it for the rhetorical presentation of this previously established meaning.

Schleiermacher, however, did not provide the last word in his analysis of hermeneutics. Further reflection, ironically, more from philosophers than theologians, has revealed that severe problems attended Schleiermacher's understanding of interpretation. In *Being and Time,* written in 1927, Martin Heidegger fundamentally altered the conceptual landscape for understanding what goes on when one interprets. Heidegger shifted the ground by a deceptively simple move drawn from the archives of classical Western philosophy. Heidegger drew upon the Aristotelian concept of the hermeneutical circle, a concept already central to Schleiermacher: we understand the part only through a grasp of the whole, yet

---

[19]See John Webster, *Holy Scripture: A Dogmatic Sketch* (Cambridge: Cambridge University Press, 2003).

we can understand the whole only through a grasp of the parts. Schleiermacher had understood the circle methodologically—as a technique used to establish the correct meaning of any text. Heidegger, however, argued that the hermeneutical circle describes the fundamental structure in which our lives unfold. Any encounter with new data, a part, arises within the context of the historical whole of our lives.

According to Heidegger such a circle provides the most fundamental context for our everyday lives. For instance, young parents may only hear the relentless crying of their young child in the middle of the night and miss the child's subtle tugging at her ear. Yet after an early morning panicked trip to Urgent Care and diagnosis of an ear infection, the next time the child cries in the night, the parents will look for—and see!—the subtle motion that shows it is her ear that hurts. They will interpret the event in light of the context of the whole of their lives (which now includes their previous experience). They will not rush out in concern for the mortal peril of their child, but provide an analgesic, hope the child will fall back asleep and proceed to call the doctor for confirmation of their diagnosis the next morning. Interpretation is not a method per se but the enclosing of new data that arises from within the whole of human lives.

The implications are immense. For Heidegger, one may not escape the concrete particularity of history. All of life occurs shaped by what has gone on before and prepares for what comes after. Interpretation provides no exception. Interpretation always takes place within a concrete historical situation. Understanding happens when new data (the part) breaks into this concrete historical context of life (the whole), becoming part of the new history (the whole) and opening the person toward new future possibilities (the part). In other words, the process of interpretation describes the basic condition of human existence. For Heidegger, "understanding is not an activity of consciousness but a condition of belonging to the world."[20]

This is heady stuff. Yet it describes the experience of the preacher very well. Any preacher has experienced what Heidegger describes in his technical, abstract, philosophical language. In the preparation of a

---

[20]Bruns, *Hermeneutics Ancient and Modern*, p. 2.

sermon, we commonly return to passages we have previously read many times, even ones carefully studied and preached before. Yet in the return to the text, suddenly we see something we had not previously seen. The text breaks into our lives differently; it speaks to us anew. Why? Has the text changed? Well, yes it has. Why else would we hear it differently? Yet, no it has not. It is still the same text we have read over and over again and we recognize it as such. The text, the part, is heard only in the context of the whole of our lives. As the whole of life changes, the part speaks to that new whole differently. Perhaps world events allowed the text to be heard anew. Perhaps a continuing education class or some pastoral experience brought forth a dynamic of the text not previously recognized. Perhaps the congregation has faced a new challenge for the faithfulness of its witness. The fact is that there is a movement from the concrete, particularity of the whole of our lives that provides the context and the means by which the part is heard, which, in turn, returns to and modifies the whole of our lives in a circular fashion. Heidegger claims that this experience characterizes all human understanding and life.

Heidegger places interpretation in a radically different context than Schleiermacher. Heidegger describes interpretation as something more basic than the construction of detailed rules to produce a highly controlled, methodological mastery of a text. Interpretation is the process of living life itself. Each encounter in life takes place within the specific circumstances of a particular history, within the unfolding of a particular narrative construction of life. This encounter is then incorporated into a new history and transforms the person. The narrative is either continued and reinforced or disrupted and broken. In the event of interpretation, the person becomes open to the future in a new way.

Heidegger's understanding of interpretation describes the event of preaching very well. Standing within a concrete situation of a local congregation, the Word is proclaimed and received or rejected, not in the abstract but within the particularity of all the history, tradition and moral commitments gathered into the sanctuary. The in-breaking of the Word becomes part of the new history, tradition and moral commitments of the congregation, transforming and opening the congregation to events of the future—a life lived in the world transformed in light of and by the Word of God. Suddenly, the specific, particular situatedness that characterizes preaching does not seem to distinguish preaching from interpretation but rather defines preaching as an exemplar of interpretation itself.

Heidegger never explicitly discussed homiletics in *Being and Time*. As a matter of fact, despite the work's importance for interpretive theory, Heidegger rarely even directly discussed hermeneutics, nor did he ever systematically develop a theory of interpretation. His later work, while remaining thoroughly hermeneutical, even abandoned the use of the term *hermeneutic*. It was the accomplishment of Heidegger's student, Hans-Georg Gadamer, in the magisterial work *Truth and Method*, to develop Heidegger's early thought into a systematic, coherent analysis of hermeneutics.

Gadamer saw how Heidegger's thought restructured the relationship between interpretation and application. After Heidegger one could no longer claim an abyss between the two. Gadamer explicitly recognized that preaching, the classical location of theological interpretation of Scripture, revealed important dynamics of what goes on in all interpretation. Gadamer recognized that Heigdegger's reframing of the hermeneutical circle challenged Schleiermacher's strong dichotomy between interpretation and application.

Gadamer's rethinking of the relationship between interpretation and application holds the key to our story about preaching as interpretation. If the theologian and preacher Schleiermacher developed an interpretative theory that excluded preaching from interpretation, the philosopher Gadamer explicitly held preaching up as a normative exemplar of the very dynamic of interpretation. Of all practices associated with reading texts, Gadamer noted that both legal judgment and preaching embraced application as central to their task:

> In both legal and theological hermeneutics there is an essential tension between the fixed text—the law or the gospel—on the one hand and, on the other, the sense arrived at by applying it at the concrete moment of interpretation, either in judgment or in preaching. A law does not exist in order to be understood historically, but to be concretized in its legal validity by being interpreted. Similarly, the gospel does not exist in order to be understood as a merely historical document, but to be taken in such a

way that it exercises its saving effect. This implies that the text, whether law or gospel, if it is to be understood properly—i.e., according to the claim it makes—must be understood at every moment, in every concrete situation, in a new and different way. Understanding here is always application.[21]

According to Gadamer's insight, application remains within interpretation. Preaching provides an archive from which application could be retrieved as an indispensable aspect of interpretation.

Preaching for Gadamer is no stepchild of interpretation. As the most concrete practice of theological hermeneutics, preaching becomes the normative guide to understanding the very dynamics of interpretation itself. The application that preaching self-consciously embraces does not exclude the practice from interpretation but rather marks preaching as interpretation par excellence.

For many within the North American culture this may seem like a curious argument. Within our own cultural context it may seem self-evident that application follows interpretation. We must, however, understand Gadamer's concept of application. Application for Gadamer is not some wooden, artificial "cut and paste" transference of a few phrases from a biblical text into a contemporary therapeutic religious psychology: "Application does not mean first understanding a given universal in itself and then afterward applying it to a concrete case."[22] Application has a more profound sense. Even before most preachers begin what they conceive of as application, a prior, more profound application—that found at a convictional level—has already taken place. How can this be so?

Gadamer's notion of application finds its origin in Heidegger's understanding of the hermeneutical circle. Interpretation happens when a text breaks into the history of an individual or group. A text is always heard within a specific, concrete situation. In interpretation a text never has a universal, abstract meaning; its "meaning" always occurs within the context of a particular history that has defined the interpreter. The enfolding of the text into this particular, concrete context possesses the structure

---

[21]Hans-Georg Gadamer, *Truth and Method,* trans. Garrett Barden and John Cumming (New York: Seabury Press, 1975), pp. 309-10.

[22]Ibid., p. 341.

of application. To understand the text, the text must connect within and to the specific history of the one to whom the text appears.

For instance, a Christian might hear Jesus' words in the Sermon on the Mount, "if you forgive men when they sin against you, your heavenly Father will also forgive you. But if you do not forgive men their sins, your Father will not forgive your sins" (Mt 6:14-15), as a generic exhortation to be nice to and therapeutically tolerant with people in general. Application takes place in the reading of the text; as a matter of fact, application *is* the reading of the text, already present in its hearing. Yet after a pastor who had become a close personal friend has to turn in his credentials for moral reasons, the parishioner-friend could hear the text as a call to intervene to support the pastor, not to remain in his charge as if nothing had happened but to work actively for the pastor's repentance and reconciliation within his family. The new situation, its application, provides a context for the text to be heard and indeed is the very hearing of the Gospel words of Jesus.

We can extend Gadamer's notion of application even a little farther. As a text reinforces or changes the direction of a person's history, it produces a new history ready to face the future. Interpretation is application because encounter with a text necessarily involves change as a person moves through time. Interpretation as application ensures that a person is never static but always on the move. Indeed, in the illustration of the pastor's moral failure, forgiving and reconciling with his brother in Christ after reading the text may open the parishioner who once heard Matthew 6:14-15 generically now to hear it also as an exhortation to deal with past conflicts within his own family differently. There is no meaning and then application; the application grows, changes direction, corrects, reproves as part of the very hearing of the text within the ongoing life of the Christian.

If application as part of interpretation takes place with the reading of Scripture, Gadamer's notion of application finds obvious resonance with the Christian practice of preaching. Like preaching, interpretation takes place within specific, given historical circumstances. Like preaching, the encounter with something outside that history, the application, modifies those circumstances, opening persons to possibilities that would otherwise be absent. Interpretation is application because to grasp the meaning of something changes the history of the one who grasps and is grasped by the text in the very act of grasping. Application arises within and out of convictions formed by particular histories, deeply rooted, largely invisible but always present.

This notion of application should not be confused with rhetorical strategizing or as building a bridge from the text to a particular situation; there is a deeper sense to this phenomenon. Dramatic examples exist to clarify this sense. When Martin Luther King Jr. read Gandhi's reading of Jesus' teaching on nonviolence, he did not "understand" the text, and then "apply" it. Rather, King stood within a particular history, the history of the oppression of African Americans in the United States. He stood at a particular time, the time of the African American struggle for civil rights. Finally, he, along with other African Americans, stood within the church as a people formed by the Scriptural teaching on nonretaliation. King's concrete historical existence opened him to grasp the gospel's teachings on nonviolence, even as those same teachings grasped him. While it is obvious that King had to apply the text to devise particular tactics to meet the challenges of the civil rights movement, this second moment of application was enabled only by a first, more profound application. This deeper application took place within King's convictions, the initial interpretation of the Gandhi text, itself formed by Gandhi's initial understanding of the Gospels, formed by his particular history within a colonized India.

Gadamer's understanding of hermeneutics vindicates preaching as a crucible for biblical interpretation. Preaching does not require that preachers understand themselves as secondary readers of the biblical text, dependent on morsels gleaned from the experts. Interpretive theory no longer legitimates the contemporary gulf between preaching and academic-historical interpretations. Preaching is an authentic place for the interpretation of the biblical text, with deep structural similarities to narrowly historical and academic readings, but one that serves a different community than that of the academy.

Why then do we often practice otherwise? The gulf between preaching and academic readings originates not within the history of the church but within the specific dynamics of the last three centuries of Western history. Both preaching and academic readings have lost a sense of interpreting the Scriptures within the particular community called the church, a polity defined by Scriptures as a distinct community in the world. By losing a sense of hearing Scriptures as members of the body of Christ, biblical readings have accommodated to the specific cultural contours of modern society. Preaching and academic readings have split at the center of this cultural narrative: preaching as reading out of the private, subjective, therapeutic side of the culture; the academic as reading out of the ruled, principle, objective side.

Embracing Gadamer's concept of application can help preachers immensely. We must not reduce our understanding of application to strategies of making the Scripture relevant for the contemporary listener's consumption. When this happens, a more profound sense of application has already occurred. Contemporary relevance often presupposes that the current status quo is natural, the only way things can be. The newness of the gospel has already lost.

Gadamer teaches us that capitulation to the reigning culture does not have to win. Interpretation is always already a different new step in the ongoing path of life. Yet this step is not always necessarily straight ahead. The more profound level of application can occur in two different directions. As the text is concretized in the particularity of our history, it will either reinforce and supplement our deepest convictions or call them into question and point in a different direction. These two possible experiences within application, or "hermeneutical moments," bear within them important possibilities for homiletics.

Comedy and Tragedy: The Two Moments of Hermeneutical Experience

It is interesting to observe responses to the classic television sitcom *I Love Lucy*. As Lucy and Ricky bumble their way into trouble after trouble, after countless fights with Fred and Ethyl, the audience nevertheless will watch with pleasure. Even amid the most severe Ricardo crisis, the tension of the conflict soothes the watcher by generating laughter. The audience knows that the ending will successfully resolve the differences that arise in the midst of each episode. The troubles of life always take place within the expectation of a harmonious outcome. The show does not deny the messiness that attends life. Indeed, episodes focus precisely on these disruptions. Yet the disruptions never deliver the final word. They are always brought within a narrative that restores and deepens relationships within the story, mirroring the hopes and convictions of the audience. Over and over again the show reinforces our fundamental convictions about the love of Lucy and Ricky, and the friendship between the Ricardos and the Muirs. The stories support our own convictions and hopes about our loves and friendships.

Such a successful resolution of a story is what makes a narrative a comedy. Comedies do not require that all go well in the midst of the story; in fact, one needs complications, events, to comprise a story in the first place. In a comedy the narrative successfully resolves whatever complications arise for the protagonist. The resolution reinforces the convictions of the audience, challenged by the story's complications. The complications even reinforce the audience's convictions more than if they had never arisen. The complications show that the underlying narrative is stronger than the disruptions. The strength of a comedy is found in its ability to absorb disruptions into a larger tale, proving the utility of the audience's convictions.

On the other hand, the events of *Romeo and Juliet* affect us completely differently. As Juliet swallows her sleeping potion, she successfully initiates her plan to unite herself with Romeo. Yet we respond with dread. The pallor of death hangs over the scene, for we are privy to information that Juliet does not have. Despite Juliet's efforts, the events spin out of control, inevitably leading toward a double suicide. As the play ends we learn not so much about Romeo and Juliet but about ourselves—our ultimate vulnerability to forces beyond ourselves, the utter contingency of life, the fragility of our deepest convictions. Shakespeare destroys the illusion that we control our lives. The tragedy shatters the presupposition that all will work out, forcing an adjustment in understanding who we are and our place in the world.

Such is the force of the tragedy. Tragedy disrupts and opens. Tragedy refuses to resolve a narrative successfully. The plot remains open, unsealed—and unsealable. Even as events flow smoothly, the calm is illusory, obscuring a deeper incongruence that threatens to overwhelm at any time. As a result, tragedy calls into question the audience's presupposition that the narrative begun in the story *should* be adequate, that in so far as the audience shares such a narrative, they themselves are vulnerable. Yet this vulnerability is also an opportunity. Tragedy reveals the frailty of the presuppositions of an audience. Having brought deep convictions to light, the difference exposed in tragedy creates the possibility of seeing anew, of discovering possibilities that had previously been masked by narratives no longer adequate. Tragedy opens to a future that comedy, by its very nature, excludes. Continuity with things as they are characterizes comedy; discontinuity characterizes tragedy.

Rom. 8:28

Comedy and tragedy exemplify the two possible moments of understanding, two very different "hermeneutical moments" found within a deep sense of application. A first moment bears the structure of a comedy. In this moment the text becomes incorporated smoothly within the present convictions of the interpreter. A synthesis occurs. This synthesis represents a new understanding in which the text now speaks within the interpreter's own perspective, enriching that perspective even as it is enfolded within it. Gadamer speaks of this event as a "fusion of horizons."[23] Both interpreter and text have a horizon, "a vantage point, a specific range of vision from which something may be observed."[24] In understanding, these two horizons become one. Out of the two, a new horizon emerges, a new unity. The text now speaks within the question posed by the horizon of the interpreter.

As in an episode of "I Love Lucy," the fusion of horizons overcomes conflict as the two horizons merge into a new understanding. The tension that arises from the incoming of the text reassures rather than disturbs. Difference loses its danger. Previous interpretive convictions prove adequate to incorporate the new text into a broader but continuous understanding. Unity finally rules. The fusion of horizons requires no fundamental shift in the self-understanding of the interpreter. A greater narrative absorbs the text within its horizon. The horizon of the interpreter, proved worthy by withstanding the horizon of the text, is now reinforced.

The fusion of horizons is like a hunch that is confirmed, a hypothesis that is validated, a conviction that is reinforced. The text becomes incor-

---

[23]See ibid., pp. 302-7.
[24]Ibid., p. 302.

porated into the convictions of the interpreter. Harmony is thereby established. The fusion of horizons enriches the interpreter's world. Narratives brought into the interpretation by the interpreter remain stable. The fusion of horizons possesses the structure of a comedy—at the end of the interpretive event, all seems right with the world. Momentary disruptions provide the texture within a broader horizon.

Perhaps no one is more aware of the truthfulness of Gadamer's words than preachers: "no text and no book speaks if it does not speak a language that reaches the other person. Thus interpretation must find the right language if it really wants to make the text speak."[25] Few experiences are worse for the preacher than seeing eyes gloss over as the sermon evaporates in mid-air before reaching the congregation. In a market-driven ecclesial economy the preacher knows that members of the audience (it is hard to speak of congregations any more) can and will go elsewhere to find preaching that will meet their perceived needs—or, worse, drop out of church altogether. It is not surprising then that contemporary preaching consistently seeks a comedic end—not through providing humor (though audiences usually enjoy a funny preacher) but through successfully fusing the horizon of the biblical text into the preexisting horizon of the audience/congregation.

We find contemporary preaching as comedy throughout the entire theological spectrum of churches in North America. The basic task of preaching is to ensure relevance by translating the biblical text into the horizon, convictions and experiences that each member possesses. The end result is to provide a biblically based answer to the questions and needs that an individual brings into the sanctuary/auditorium through fusing the biblical text into the experience of the hearer. The great twentieth-century liberal theologian Paul Tillich expressed such a conviction. In the process he sounds very much like an evangelical preacher describing a homiletical strategy for a seeker-sensitive service:

> A large part of the congregation at the Sunday services came from outside the Christian circle in the most radical sense of the phrase. For them, a sermon in traditional Biblical terms would have had no meaning. Therefore, I was obliged to seek a language to which the Biblical and ecclesi-

---

[25]Ibid., p. 397.

astical terminology points. In this situation, an "apologetic" type of sermon has been developed.[26]

Tillich is quite clear: the biblical, ecclesial language lies outside the horizon of the congregation, making them unable to hear the biblical words. Therefore, preaching must translate the biblical language into the horizon of the audience so that they might understand their experience in Christian terms. The fusion of horizons takes place in the melding of the translated biblical conceptuality into the previously existing horizon of the hearers, Christian and non-Christian alike. The sermon seeks to reinforce and uphold each attendee's basic convictions, bringing in an experience of "the Christ" in order to enrich the lives of all present as they struggle through their daily existence. [27] Preaching here is characterized by the fusion of horizons. It therefore has the structure of a comedy.

Contemporary homiletician David Buttrick actively advocates for this comedic tradition of preaching. Buttrick understands the purpose of preaching to "name God" in the world of human experience. He writes, "Preaching that dares to name God in connection with a wide range of human experience will shape in congregational consciousness a live hermeneutic for scripture. When we name God with the world, then biblical stories become meaningful."[28] The vision here is thoroughly comedic: the hearer's horizon provides the field into which homiletics places the biblical stories. The preacher seeks to enrich the hearer's horizon and ensure the meaningfulness of the biblical witness.

Both Tillich and Buttrick, of course, represent a mainline, liberal theological perspective. Yet the commitment to comedic moment in preaching is not confined to mainline churches. Contemporary evangelical preaching has actually been much more effective at fusing the horizon of the biblical text into the horizon of the contemporary hearer than the mainline churches. This is perhaps most exemplified in the phrase, echoed throughout evangelical Christianity, of biblically based, need-centered preaching. The phrase exemplifies the same apologetic, comedic

---

[26]Paul Tillich, quoted in Campbell, *Preaching Jesus*, p. 42.
[27]See Campbell's excellent analysis in *Preaching Jesus*, pp. 29-62.
[28]David Buttrick, *Homiletic: Moves and Structures* (Philadelphia: Fortress, 1987), p. 19.

structure of preaching as Tillich, except it aims at the middle class, while Tillich was trying to reach the secular elite. Contemporary evangelical preaching often translates the Scriptures into the "needs" of its intended audience, the private, personal, therapeutic horizon of its North American hearers. Such folk search for purpose as they struggle with the bumps of their individual and familial lives. Evangelical preachers master the art of absorbing the biblical text within the convictions that the hearers bring with them into the sanctuary/auditorium. One then can get an audience to fill in the blanks to answer questions arising out of their experience. Scriptural allusions enrich their preexisting horizon with Christian imagery and solutions. Preaching thereby christianizes the horizons with which the audience entered worship in the first place. Again, such preaching bears the structure of a comedy: the disruptions caused by the reading of the biblical text are ultimately dissipated as the horizon of the text becomes fused into the horizon of the congregation/audience. As a result, the fundamental convictions of the hearers remain intact and even reinforced and reassured.

The comedic moment in preaching offers several obvious strengths. By definition the Scriptures bear a relevance to individual lives. In Gadamer's terms the preaching reaches the hearers. The text speaks forth in a language that is grasped by its hearers. The proclaimed Word is woven into the texture of the convictions that the hearers bring to the hearing. Speaking apart from the audience, the text speaks to them as well. The Scripture enriches their horizon and brings the Scriptures into their lives in a manner that informs their everyday life.

A certain pleasure results—everyone likes a happy ending! Disruptions find their way to resolution without having to deny that they are there in the first place. Preaching to fuse the horizon of the text within the horizon of the hearers addresses tensions that already exist in life but works through them. The tension-release allows people to feel challenged from the fact that the tension was addressed, but confident that it can be surmounted. The sermon successfully seals the text as an answer to the question that already exists in the horizon of the hearer. Hearers may come away energized, fed from the preached Word, soothed and ready to come back again next Sunday to consume more of the product that the Scriptures have to offer.

What Preacher Could Ask for Anything More?

One major problem exists in the homiletical attempt to fuse the biblical
text into the experiential horizon of the hearers formed by contemporary
cultural convictions—the preaching never challenges the deepest convictions, the most profound narratives, of the hearers. Comedic preaching never opens the hearers to the genuinely new, the possibility of a
different narrative in which they can live their lives outside a certain
Christianized version of the standard story that sustains the society at
large, that of an autonomous individual searching for their personal
good. Such preaching never calls forth a conversion of the hearer in the
most profound sense. In the terms of A. D. Nock, such an approach encourages adherence, not conversion.[29] The biblical text, not the hearer,
becomes converted. Given that the horizons of the hearer are usually
shaped by narratives provided by and supporting the society at large, the
comedic hermeneutic of preaching leads to believers who share the
identical convictions of the society but possess a value-added dimension—Jesus in one's heart or a personal relationship with God or some
other life-enriching experience that helps one to exist as a member of
the society as it is.

Of course, with preaching that reinforces the already present convictions of individual believers, the church as a people will also exist as a
value-added subgroup. Rather than a "contrast society" in continuity
with earliest Christianity, a positive alternative community witnessing to
the God of Israel and Jesus Christ within the world, the comedic hermeneutic generates a group who claims an enriching perspective to enhance participation within the North American society at large.[30] Despite
its claim to special, even exclusive, knowledge, such a church can only
exist deeply assimilated to the contours of its host society. This is precisely what we find in the contemporary church. Rodney Clapp has
called this "the full Constantinianization of the church." Clapp writes:

> The Constantinian church is *by definition* reactive and reflexive to the sur-
> rounding culture. It completely forgets the church's own culture-forming

---

[29]See A. D. Nock, *Conversion: The Old and New in Religion from Alexander to Augustine of
Hippo* (Oxford: Clarendon Press, 1933).

[30]For the early church as a "contrast society," see Gerhard Lohfink, *Jesus and Community* (Philadelphia: Fortress, 1984), esp. p. 72.

and sustaining capabilities. It denies any real tension between the church and the world; it overlooks the biblical awareness of Christians as nomads and resident aliens who will never be completely at home in a fallen world—even an affluent and exceedingly comfortable fallen world. And it aligns the church with power, against those out of power.[31]

Without a hermeneutic that can challenge the horizon of the hearers by the horizon of the Scriptures, the church can only respond to the society in which it sojourns and will always be captive to the role that the host society will permit it to play.

The hermeneutical event as a comedy, the fusion of horizons, however, is not the only possible hermeneutical moment. Understanding as application can also entail a moment of tragedy, a moment in which our convictions are cast open rather than sealed shut. Gadamer describes this moment as "hermeneutical experience."[32] Interpretation always entails the interpretation of something else, something other. We encounter this "other" in experience. The experience of the other can be, by its very nature, unsettling. We don't choose what we experience; experience happens *to us*. In experience we do not so much encounter something new as much as something new, something outside our control, encounters us, for which we must now account. As pastors can discover when a mundane board meeting suddenly exposes a rift in the congregation, all our experience runs the grave risk of disconfirming what we have known, rendering cherished convictions obsolete. Gadamer writes, "experience in this sense inevitably involves many disappointments of one's expectations and only thus is experience acquired. That experience refers chiefly to painful and disagreeable experiences does not mean that we are being especially pessimistic, but can be seen directly from its nature. Only through negative instances do we acquire new experiences."[33]

Experience in this sense always reveals to us the limitations of our horizons. It demands that we alter the horizons in order to account for the new experience. Hermeneutical experience thus reveals *my* inadequacy,

---

[31]Rodney Clapp, *A Peculiar People: The Church as Culture in a Post-Christian Society* (Downers Grove, Ill.: InterVarsity Press, 1996), p. 39.
[32]Gadamer, *Truth and Method*, pp. 346-62.
[33]Ibid., p. 356.

the need for *my* transformation. Hermeneutical experience exposes the delusions I lived in before my confrontation with the other. In hermeneutical experience the horizon of the text does not fuse with the horizon of the interpreter. Rather, the horizon of the text confronts the horizon of the interpreter, challenges it, unmasks it and demands a transformation of the interpreter by absorbing the interpreter's horizon within the otherness of the text. Seen through the moment of hermeneutical experience, understanding a text looks much differently: "To understand a text is not only to grasp its meaning; it is to understand the claim that it has on us. Most often this claim is critical in the strong sense, as when a text exposes to us . . . the conceptual frameworks we inhabit and to which we appeal when we try to make sense of things."[34]

Hermeneutical experience, therefore, names a tragic moment in understanding. As in tragedy, confrontation with the limits of one's horizons, convictions called into question, can be painful. Simply stated, hermeneutical experience shatters—like watching *Romeo and Juliet* immediately before proposing. Yet hermeneutical experience is not merely negative; it also opens. The tragic hermeneutical moment casts light on our self-understanding in a way the fusion of horizons cannot. Insight and self-recognition become inescapable. Hermeneutical experience places our horizons in question so that we might find answers that would otherwise be unthinkable. Whereas the fusion of horizons enfolds a text into our past horizons, hermeneutical experience opens our horizons to the future. "Understanding a text means being resituated not only in relation to the text but with respect to the present and future."[35]

Alasdair McIntyre has called this tragic hermeneutical moment an "epistemological crisis."[36] Unfortunately, such crises arise within the everyday experience of us all. Dramatically, a wife unsuspectingly comes home to find a note that her husband of fifteen years has suddenly left her for his secretary. Suddenly her husband's "late nights at work" take

---

[34]Bruns, *Hermeneutics: Ancient and Modern*, p. 183.

[35]Ibid., p. 194.

[36]Alasdar McIntyre, "Epistemological Crises, Dramatic Narrative, and the Philosophy of Science," in *Why Narrative? Readings in Narrative Theology,* ed. Stanley Hauerwas and L. Gregory Jones (Eugene, Ore.: Wipf & Stock, 1997), pp. 138-57.

on a new significance. McIntyre writes about such occasions:

> What they [those who experience such events] took to be evidence point-
> ing unambiguously in some one direction now turns out to have been
> equally susceptible of rival interpretations. Such a discovery is often pa-
> ralysing, and were we all of us all of the time to have to reckon with the
> multiplicity of possible interpretations, social life as we know it could
> scarcely continue.[37]

McIntyre's contribution, however, is to develop this tragic hermeneutical moment—and its resolution—in terms of narrative. For McIntyre,
narrative is absolutely fundamental to understand human activity. Only
through stories can we make sense of what people do. Underlying narratives provide the context, the horizon, for intelligible human activity.
Staying up all night long in order to write feverishly for two hours in a
closed room the following morning makes little sense unless one knows
the underlying story of a college student trying to do well on final exams
so that she or he might get into medical school. Knowing the story gives
a context—and thus intelligibility—to the student's actions. Narratives
provide a framework, what Gadamer calls the horizon, for understanding someone's activities and life.

An epistemological crisis occurs when a person's narrative account is
no longer an adequate account for the data at hand—the note from the
adulterous husband just will not fit coherently within the betrayed wife's
narrative of her husband as a "hard-working family man trying to support his family." The collapse of a previously held narrative brings with
it a new and often awkward self-consciousness and vulnerability—a
woman who undergoes such an experience will often ask, How could I
have been so blind? She might be very tentative before she trusts a male
again. An epistemological crisis grants a self-knowledge that otherwise
would escape our own understanding of ourself. As in tragedy, we stand
exposed in front of new data. The new data interrogates us; we don't
interrogate it.

For McIntyre, however, an epistemological crisis is not terminal.
Again, narrative is the key. A person may resolve an epistemological crisis. A person may overcome the tragic hermeneutical moment by con-

---

[37]Ibid., pp. 138-39.

structing a new, more adequate, narrative. For this narrative to resolve the crisis, it must enable

> the agent to understand *both* how he or she could intelligibly have held his or her original beliefs *and* how he or she could have been so drastically misled by them. The narrative in terms of which he or she at first understood and ordered experience is itself made into the subject of an enlarged narrative.[38]

The unfortunate wife can make sense of her husband's sudden departure by seeing within it a wider web of deception he has woven and the extreme care he took to conceal the truth from her. The tragic moment, therefore, plays a positive role in understanding. It provides the occasion for the "construction and reconstruction of more adequate narratives and forms of narrative."[39] Tragic though her situation is, the wife may now live more truthfully, knowing that her husband was a chronic liar and an adulterous cheat rather than responding to him as a faithful, sacrificial worker for the benefit of the family. Her hope for the future comes only through the confrontation with the truth, painful though it is. The tragic moment allows her to live within a new narrative context that provides possibilities for a good life outside the deceptive practices of her ex-husband.

The tragic moment in understanding, or an epistemological crisis, is not fun to experience, but it nevertheless serves two very helpful functions for human life. First, it reveals the narratives that form, guide and shape human lives. Often these narratives remain submerged or even denied, hidden but actively determining life and behavior. A person may be an alcoholic without ever admitting it to him- or herself—an epistemological crisis takes away the false comfort of an inadequate narrative. Second, the tragic moment provides the occasion for the construction of a truthful narrative, one in which the individual is incorporated into the new data or text rather than vice versa. This new narrative can more adequately and truthfully account for the experience of the person, and thus open possibilities for the future that otherwise would have been denied. To speak theologically, the tragic moment of application provides

---

[38]Ibid., pp. 140-41.
[39]Ibid., p. 142.

the opportunity for repentance—a personal turning arising out of genuine self-knowledge—and conversion—the incorporation of human life within the biblical narrative of God's redemption of all creation through Jesus Christ. The negative hermeneutical moment therefore provides a gift that otherwise would leave humans to stagnate, without any possibility for transformation.

Whereas preachers have warmly embraced the comedic fusion of horizons, they have shied away from a tragic moment where the biblical text confronts and calls into question the horizon of the congregation. Perhaps revivalistic preaching, in its attempt to awaken a sense of sin in the individual, comes closest to preaching to bring about a rupture in the horizon of the hearer. Yet, as will become apparent in chapter two, revivalistic preaching, with its emphasis on the religious subjectivity of the individual, itself translates the biblical narrative into the life of the believer, though with an intensity not found in more genteel Christian settings.

Understanding why preachers have been reticent to embrace the tragic hermeneutical moment in preaching is not difficult. The tragic moment is a moment of vulnerability—for the congregation and the preacher. First, there is the risk that the hearer will not hear the Word at all—the congregation may not have ears to hear nor eyes to see. Too many irrelevant sermons or "I don't get it" responses will surely send the early twenty-first-century religious consumer to the next church down the road so that their "needs" might be met. Second, the pain of an epistemological crisis, while ultimately helpful, initially sends shock waves through individuals and congregations. Will the congregation wait it out, making it through the destruction of their horizon to see anew another day? Or will they receive the biblical text as a violation of their horizon, seal themselves off, never to return to the sanctuary again? The self-preservation instinct of preachers is quite large, for with those members goes also the funding that pays the preacher's salary, not to mention the stability of the church. As Stanley Hauerwas writes:

> The ministry seems captured in our time by people who are desperately afraid they might actually be caught, at one point or another in their ministry, with a conviction that might curtail future ambition. They therefore see their task as to "manage" their congregations by specializing in the politics of agreement by always being agreeable. The preaching such a

ministry produces is designed to reinforce our presumed agreements since a "good church" is one without conflict. You cannot preach about abortion, suicide, or war because those are such controversial subjects—better to concentrate on "insights," since they do so little work for the actual shaping of our lives and occasion no conflict.[40]

In today's cultural environment, preaching is used to calm conflict, not produce it. *- To comfort the afflicted as opposed to afflicting the comfortable.*

Yet when we accept God's call to become preachers of the gospel, we accept as well God's call to speak truthfully even if conflict results, even if at times it causes conflict with the world, especially as it has already possessed us. Again Hauerwas reminds us:

> The enemy, who is often enough ourselves, does not like to be reminded that the narratives that constitute our lives are false. Moreover, you had better be ready for a fierce encounter-offensive as well as be prepared to take some casualties. God has not promised us safety, but rather participation in an adventure called the Kingdom.[41]

Embracing the tragic hermeneutic of preaching brings the possibility of conflict. Yet conflict is necessary for conversion, the world's, the congregation's—and the preacher's. The tragic hermeneutical moment in preaching provides the opportunity for a genuine shift in the horizon of the congregation—a shift of allegiances from those of the society at large to those of the church in submission to Christ. The tragic moment unseals the congregation so that they might find their lives in the biblical narrative, rather than absorbing the biblical narrative into theirs. The consistent in-breaking of the Word in proclamation can re-form a congregation into an alternative community, Christianly distinct from the world around them, a particular people whose witness lies in the Scriptural horizon of their communal life. As the biblical narrative forms a distinct, embodied culture, the congregation then may provide resources that the world otherwise would never have opportunity to see. As such, preaching to an epistemological crisis can be used by the Spirit to form the church into "a kingdom of priests, a holy nation" (Ex 19:6; cf. 1 Pet 2:9).

---

[40]Stanley Hauerwas, "No Enemy, No Christianity: Preaching Between 'Worlds,' " in *Sanctify Them in the Truth: Holiness Exemplified* (Nashville: Abingdon, 1998), p. 195.
[41]Ibid., p. 199.

This tragic hermeneutic, a homiletic of repentance and conversion, is what I will embrace and explore in this book. The questions I pursue, therefore, focus on a developing a countercultural homiletic: How do we transcend the apologetic, comedic homiletic of contemporary North American Christianity in order to lead the congregation to an epistemological crisis so that God the Father might form a peculiar people through Jesus Christ by power of the Spirit? How might we engage the narrative horizon of a contemporary congregation, yet move them to faithfulness to the God of Israel, the God of Jesus Christ, as narrated in the Christian Scripture? In developing this homiletic of repentance, how do we keep the scandal on the cross rather than on the preacher? How do we weave the biblical story so as to form the church to live as an alternative community, a peculiar people living amid the nations today?

The next task necessary is to dig out the narrative horizons that shape much of North American Christianity today—horizons that have moved worldwide through the active American missionary enterprise of the past century. Brought to light, the preacher may address directly these simple but deeply embedded narrative convictions without capitulating to them. Such a moment of historical and theological analysis can open the way to a new possibility, the formation of faithful community living within God's story of the restoration of all creation through Jesus Christ.

2

ECLIPSING THE
BIBLICAL NARRATIVE

The Narrative Contours of
North American Christianity

Preaching is always a concrete practice. No homiletical instruction can form abstract, universal principles to meet every situation for every congregation. A book on preaching must address its concrete setting—this book is written within the horizon of North American Christianity, particularly within its evangelical form. As the church rapidly moves into the twenty-first century, though, "North American evangelical Christianity" is not just found on the North American continent but has become an international phenomenon. The missionary zeal of the twentieth-century Protestant missionary movement has spread evangelicalism into all corners of the world. Even as it becomes indigenous within these new settings, a very particular narrative substructure has largely determined this specific historical form of Christianity.

The argument of this chapter is historical, cultural and theological. I believe that "American Christianity" or, as Harold Bloom has called it, "American religion" arose at a time when a fundamental shift occurred within the underlying narrative horizon of the church's life and practice.[1] Whereas the church had historically lived out of the biblical story of God's promise to Abraham and Sarah fulfilled in Jesus and made mani-

---

[1]See Harold Bloom, *American Religion: The Emergence of the Post-Christian Nation* (New York: Simon & Schuster, 1992).

fest in the life of the church, this new narrative placed the individual's movement from sin to salvation to service at its center. As the traditional Christian typology between Israel and the church collapsed, a new type for Israel arose—the modern American nation-state. These two distinct narratives—an individual's "personal salvation" and the moral mission of the nation-state—have become deeply embedded within the cultural horizons of North America.

This is the narrative tradition into which contemporary preaching has sought to translate the biblical text. Mainstream North American culture has formed preachers to interpret the Scriptures within and for the space afforded by these dominant narratives. Preachers constantly feel pressure to make market forces their friend, thus conserving the culture's deepest narratives. Since the customer is always right, the church in North America tends to reflect divisions that exist within the society, divisions that arise out of its underlying cultural narratives—the divisions of the political right and left, or divisions of economic class, ethnicity and race. To preach in North America is to address this context, one way or another.

We could analyze such narrative substructures in order to become more sophisticated in accommodation to it for market reasons. Yet a different, theological, ecclesial reason exists to engage this history. We will engage these narratives to read against them, to understand ourselves in relationship to the Scriptural narrative. Out of the difference between the North American narratives and the biblical narrative, a tragic homiletic might engage a congregation to create a space for a new social formation, a distinct people formed by the biblical story. Such a community could live shaped by the gospel through the power of the Holy Spirit, not by the political right or the left, or by a consumerism that merely reproduces the demographic fissures of the contemporary society.

Much is at stake for the church in the story we will tell. Profound consequences have befallen, and continue to befall, the life of the church as a result of the narrative accommodation of the church to its North American setting. These consequences deeply endanger the future of the church's life and witness. To understand this danger, we must retell the story of the formation of the church in North America through its preaching. A convenient place to begin this story is in post-Reformation, Western Europe.

The Eclipse of Biblical Narrative and the Birth of American Christianity

The seventeenth and eighteenth centuries brought about massive changes in the culture, politics and theology of Western Europe. Christians found themselves unable to unify on the basis of the Protestant principal of Scripture alone. The emergence of a new political organization, the modern liberal state, caused social turmoil and offered itself as the solution to the problems that it caused.[2] Thinkers searched for an objective, universal reason to serve as a foundation for a society's politics. If this objective foundation was established, any rational person might voluntarily assent to the rule of the state that sought to protect access to this foundation for all those under its discipline.[3]

A new agenda arose that Christian thinkers/preachers tried to address. For Christianity to be true, it was thought, the faith must conform to a prior, universally accessible truth. Scriptures became understood as a source, a universal, objective foundation, for the construction of a Christian theology.[4]

This shift held massive implications for the understanding of Scriptures. These implications were not immediately apparent to those who engaged in the transformation. Drawing on Karl Barth, Hans Frei documented this shift as an "eclipse of biblical narrative."[5] Barth had earlier observed that at the end of the seventeenth century, an "unfortunate habit of Western thought" assumed that the Scriptures stood or fell by

---

[2]See William Cavanaugh, " 'A Fire Strong Enough to Consume the House': The Wars of Religion and the Rise of the State," *Modern Theology* 11 (1995): 397-420; see also William Cavanaugh, *Theopolitical Imagination: Discovering the Liturgy as a Political Act in an Age of Global Capitalism* (Edinburgh: T & T Clark, 2002).

[3]For a anthropological and political analysis of this position see Talal Asad, *Formations of the Secular: Christianity, Islam, Modernity* (Stanford, Calif.: Stanford University Press, 2003), and *Genealogies of Religion: Discipline and Reasons of Power in Christianity and Islam* (Baltimore: Johns Hopkins University Press, 1993); for an analysis of how foundationalism effect theological endeavors, see Stanley J. Grenz and John R. Franke, *Beyond Foundationalism: Shaping Theology in a Postmodern Context* (Louisville, Ky.: Westminster John Knox Press, 2001), pp. 28-37; see also Nancey Murphy, *Beyond Liberalism and Fundamentalism: How Modern and Postmodern Philosophy Set the Theological Agenda* (Harrisburg, Penn.: Trinity Press International, 1996), pp. 11-35.

[4]See Murphy, *Beyond Liberalism and Fundamentalism,* pp. 15-19.

[5]For much of the following analysis see Hans Frei, *The Eclipse of Biblical Narrative: A Study in Eighteenth and Nineteenth Century Hermeneutics* (New Haven, Conn.: Yale University Press, 1974).

whether or not it was history.[6] A massive bifurcation of the church resulted. Liberalism attempted to purify the Bible historically through the
methodological application of objective reason. In response, a new
theological orthodoxy arose that denied such a need. This group argued
that objective reason shows that such a task of purification is unnecessary—reason shows that the Bible contains nothing but history.[7] Both
sides assumed that what really mattered theologically was the objective
history contained within or behind the biblical text. History, as recon-
structed by rational historians, provided the foundation for the life of the
church. Such a move denied the church's own narrative-formed life as
the legitimate context for reading Scripture.

Hans Frei expanded Barth's insight through extensive cultural-historical-
theological analysis. Frei's work, however, is difficult to access. In the
words of one of his students, "The tortured syntax so often evident in
his prose seems to be matched only by the profundity of insight which
that very syntax seemed at once to promise and yet also so vexingly to
withhold."[8] Yet his thesis is extremely important to understand the distinct nature of Protestant Christianity in North America. Frei's analysis
uncovers an underlying narrative structure that established the horizon
for much of the homiletical performance of the Scriptures within a North
American setting.

According to Frei, traditional, precritical Christian readings of the
Scriptures had presupposed a unified narrative structure of the Bible. A
sense of the Scriptures as a unitary story held together the literal and fig-
urative/typological sense of the Scriptures. Christians read the Scriptures
to find themselves within its pages. The Bible presented an overarching
theological narrative. The narrative framework of the biblical story itself
provided the Christian pattern of meaning for all of life. An individual
read the Scriptures in order to incorporate the world, oneself and, for
preachers, the congregation into the biblical story.[9] Much like seeing

---

[6]Karl Barth, *Church Dogmatics: The Doctrine of Creation* 3.1 (London: T & T Clark, 1958), p. 82.
[7]Ibid.
[8]George Hunsinger, "Afterword," in Hans W. Frei, *Theology and Narrative: Selected Essays,* ed.
George Hunsinger and William Placher (New York: Oxford University Press, 1993), p. 236.
[9]Frei summarizes the shift in biblical interpretation in the seventeenth and eighteenth century:
"It is no exaggeration to say that all across the theological spectrum the great reversal had
taken place; interpretation was a matter of fitting the biblical story into another world with

oneself within a previously drawn painting, the skilled Christian interpreter was to discover him- or herself and their contemporary world within the pages of the biblical text.

According to Frei, all this had radically changed. The shift began in the seventeenth century and conquered the whole Western intellectual landscape in the eighteenth and nineteenth centuries. Theologians and preachers lost the sense of the Scriptures as a story in and of itself. Instead, the Bible was seen as a source for history—an objective history on which to assert Christianity's universal, rational truthfulness. The Scriptures were read to establish something behind the text—the objective universal ground of history.

The meaning of the Scriptures became separated from the Scripture's words. The Scriptures themselves presented no patterns but pointed instead to patterns found in history. Such an understanding radically undercut traditional typological reading of the Scriptures, typological readings that had held the Scriptures, Old and New Testaments, together as the normative resource for the life of the church.[10]

Scriptures, above all, were seen to refer to something behind the text that could be excavated from it through the application of a proper rational method, as seen, for instance, in Schleiermacher's hermeneutic. Theologians and preachers understood Scriptures to refer to a reality in history that lay behind their words, in either individual or communal experience of God or factual events or revealed theological propositions to which one could then rationally assent.[11]

The Bible became a source, not a text. Theologians and preachers understood the Scriptures as a platform on which they could either access experiences of the divine or build theological systems and propositions to nurture the life of their congregations and call unbelievers to faith. Such an understanding separated Scripture from the life of a peculiar people called the church in order to hand it over to individuals to induce

---

another story rather than incorporating that world into the biblical story" (*Eclipse of Biblical Narrative*, p. 130).

[10]See the works of Henri De Lubac, especially *Medieval Exegesis*, 2 vols. (Grand Rapids: Eerdmans, 1998-2000); and *Scripture in the Tradition* (New York: Crossroad, 2000).

[11]See Murphy, *Beyond Liberalism & Fundamentalism*, see also George A. Lindbeck, *The Nature of Doctrine: Religion and Theology in a Postliberal Age* (Louisville, Ky.: Westminster John Knox Press, 1984), from whom Murphy develops her analysis.

inward, personal experiences or rational assent.

Preachers faced a new challenge in using the Scriptures in preaching. The Scriptures no longer provided a place for the individual and congregation to find themselves within its pages through typological readings. One could only go behind the text into the past with a technical historical method. Such a method taught the preacher to find the text's reference in either a factual event or a true proposition or in some sort of religious experience. Once establishing this universal base, the preacher could cross into the contemporary context through a "hermeneutical bridge."

The Scriptures no longer bore immediate relevance to the life of the church as the ongoing story we continue to live in. The preacher had to make the Scriptural meaning relevant by a method of abstraction from its narrative context and then a reapplication into the contemporary setting to shape the life of individuals within the congregation.

Such an understanding undercut the narrative quality of Scripture for preaching. The Scriptures, now read as a source, became vulnerable to co-optation by other narratives. The contemporary context, not the biblical narrative nor some objective spot outside of history, determined the Scriptures' meaning within this new system.[12]

Protestant evangelical orthodoxy was not immune to these shifts. The evangelical Christian life story of individual salvation became abstracted from the wider framework of the biblical story and the life of the church. For evangelicals another narrative was available to provide the narrative context of the interpretation of Scripture in preaching. The story of the individual's salvation stood ready to replace the biblical narrative in structuring the life of the Christian.

The profound shift entailed here is important. The biblical story begins with God creating the cosmos from nothing and ends with God's restoration of this creation through the faithfulness of Jesus Christ. Its central actor is God; creation provides the setting for its story. The plot is simple yet all-encompassing. The scriptural narrative moves from creation in it primal harmonious goodness back toward nothingness

---

[12]Perhaps the most famous critique of this tendency found within nineteenth-century German biblical scholarship is Albert Schweitzer, *The Quest of the Historical Jesus: A Critical Study of Its Progress from Reimarus to Wrede* (New York: Macmillan, 1961).

through sin and into its final restoration in the second coming of Christ. Within this story God per se does not act in history. History, though distinct from God, nevertheless occurs in God. God is the One in whom we "live, and move, and have our being" (Acts 17:28).

In light of deep cultural and political changes, the Scriptures became read within a very different story line. In this new narrative the interior life of the individual, not creation, provided the setting for the story. Creation provides a context for God's acts in history, but history must therefore move outside of God, activated by its human or nonhuman actors. A secular realm outside of God develops.[13]

Each individual became the story's central actor; God may play a supporting role within the story of each—based upon the will of the individual. God may be called on by faith to act within the life of the individual, but only to move the individual to the person's own end. As a result, the movement of the story focuses on the life of the individual, as he or she moves from sin to awakening to justification to service and sanctification, and ultimately to heavenly glorification. As Frei summarized, readers read the Scriptures "to present experience in the history of the soul's conversion and perfection."[14]

Instead of God's story of the redemption of all creation, the Bible was narrowed to the story of personal salvation. In this new evangelical piety, "What is real, and what therefore the Christian really lives, is his [the individual's] own pilgrimage."[15] The individual turns to the Scriptures for assurance that he or she really is living within this spiritual path that leads to individual eternal bliss in heaven.[16] The cult of the individual arises, now with full biblical warrant. The life of the church fades into the background. The church becomes a service provider to provide the opportunity for salvation that each and every individual needs.

---

[13]"Once, there was no 'secular.' . . . Instead there was the single community of Christendom, with its dual aspects of *sacerdotium* and *regnum*. The *saeculum*, in the medieval era, was not a space, a domain—but a time—the interval between fall and *eschaton* where coercive justice, private property and impaired reason must make shift to cope with the unredeemed effects of sinful humanity" (John Milbank, *Theology and Social Theory: Beyond Secular Reason* [Oxford: Blackwell, 1990], p. 9).

[14]Frei, *Eclipse of Biblical Narrative*, p. 152.

[15]Ibid., p. 154.

[16]Ibid.

The Eclipse of Biblical Narrative and Puritan Preaching

Frei's theological and cultural analysis tells the story of the demise of biblical narrative within the lofty, seemingly disembodied, realm of European intellectual history. Yet Frei's story is of extreme importance for understanding the rise and nature of American Christianity.

The origins of a European-based society in North America overlapped chronologically with this eclipse of biblical narrative. The main transmitters of this narrative shift in North America were not European intellectuals, through whom Frei tends to tell the story, but preachers who lived in North America, particularly Puritan preachers. One way of understanding the great experiment in European-settled North America is to see it as an attempt to build a righteous Christian nation that provides individual freedom so that an individual may move, through faith, from sin to salvation. Indeed, these evangelical narratives have profoundly overdetermined the theological horizons of American ecclesial and national life.

Puritan preaching was extremely important in the formation of the narrative horizons of North American Protestants. Harry Stout has shown the centrality of Puritan preachers in colonial New England. Preachers had unbridled authority to proclaim the Word of God to the whole of the society: "The ministers enjoyed awesome powers in New England society; they alone could speak for God in public assemblies of the entire congregation. Their sermons were the only voice of authority that congregations were pledged to obey unconditionally."[17] In a society without the white noise of television, radios, e-mails, cell phones, pagers, spin doctors or political advertisements, the words of the preacher in the sermon bore unchallenged ability to shape the lives of all within the society.

Twice each Sunday New Englanders heard "regular sermons," salvation sermons. Stout has read extensively these Puritan regular sermons, both published and unpublished, over five generations. While rhetorical conventions changed, Stout found that Puritan salvation preaching remained remarkably consistent in their narrative structure.

---

[17]Harry S. Stout, *The New England Soul: Preaching and Religious Culture in Colonial New England* (New York: Oxford University Press, 1986), p. 19.

The regular sermons were basically oral expositions of the "covenant of grace." Quite simply, the minister narrated the sequence of an individual's movement from sin to awakening to one's sinfulness, to justification and assurance, to service and sanctification, or as Stout summarizes, with appropriate homiletical alliteration, a "sin-salvation-service" sequence. This narrative structure provided a basic narrative framework for the interpretation of Scripture. As Stout writes:

> The sin-salvation-service formula was merely the skeleton around which the preacher crafted his discourse. To flesh out that skeleton, he had recourse to a broad range of tropes and metaphors drawn from Scripture and from the common experiences of the listeners. . . . Ministers would ransack the Scriptures for images and analogies that could hold up obscure spiritual truths to the apprehension and appreciation of their listeners.[18]

The sin-salvation-service narrative provided a fundamental framework for the interpretation of Scripture. Scriptures became translated directly into the lives of individuals as each one moved through this earthly life toward their own individual eternal end.

Sunday after Sunday, week after week, year after year, even generation after generation, the same underlying narrative provided the interpretative horizon for reading and hearing the Scriptures. The narrative of Scripture was found in the order of salvation. Salvation, however, was not understood as individual participation within the biblical narrative that told how the God of creation made a promise to Abraham that was fulfilled in Jesus in order to bring about a witness in the life of the church as a foretaste of the new creation. Instead, salvation was limited to a story of the individual moving from sin to salvation to service in preparation for eternity in heaven. The spiritual movement of an individual's life became deeply encoded as *the* meaning of Scripture within the emerging European-based North American culture.

We find ourselves here at the bedrock of American Christianity—the eclipse of biblical narrative. The Bible became the story of God saving the individual soul, not God the Father's reclamation of all of creation from sin and death through the Son by the power of the Spirit. The in-

---

[18]Ibid, p. 43.

terpretative horizon for reading the Scripture became the life of the individual, into whose personal life God could come to grant forgiveness and assurance, and empower individual Christians for a life of service in the world. Preaching over and over encoded the Bible into the story of an individual's awakening to his or her own sinfulness as the precondition for repentance and faith. The goal was to empower an individual to live for God within the society.

American Protestants experienced this narrative within the very framework of their lives. Jonathan Edwards in *A Faithful Narrative of the Surprising Work of God* validated the covenant of grace as an empirical, psychological reality. Edwards interviewed those who had experienced awakening within his local parish. He discovered a consistent pattern, a pattern that, not surprisingly, followed the identical narrative structure of the Puritan salvation sermon. Edwards discovered that individuals narrated their spiritual journey as beginning with an awakening. Edwards wrote, "Persons are first awakened with a sense of their miserable condition by nature, the danger they are in of perishing eternally, and that it is of great importance to them that they speedily escape and get into a better state."[19] Such movement into spiritual bliss was not easily experienced but accompanied by spiritual despair. Edwards found that

> there is a very great variety as to the degree of fear and trouble that persons are exercised with before they obtain any comfortable evidences of pardon and acceptance with God. . . . The awful apprehensions persons have had of their misery have, for the most part, been increasing the nearer they have approached to deliverance, though they often pass through many changes in the frame and circumstances of their minds.[20]

The movement of the individual into the covenant of grace was fraught with danger.

Individuals were, according to Edwards, often tempted to give up their struggle as they moved through various psychological states, from hope to despair:

---

[19]Jonathan Edwards, *A Faithful Narrative of the Surprising Work of God in Northampton*, in *The Works of Jonathan Edwards: The Great Awakening*, ed. C. C. Goen (New Haven, Conn.: Yale University Press, 1972), 4:160.
[20]Ibid., p. 161.

Thus they wander about from mountain to hill, seeking rest and finding none: when they are beat out of one refuge they fly to another, till they are, as it were, debilitated, broken, and subdued with legal humblings; in which God gives them a conviction of their own utter helplessness and insufficiency and discovers the true remedy.[21]

The individual's knowledge of Christ provides the means out of their own inner turmoil that arises from their legal distresses. At this point the individual usually experienced a time of quiet and rest. Ultimately, among the elect,

grace seems sometimes first to appear after legal humiliation . . . in earnest longings of soul after God and Christ, to know God, to love him, to be humbled before him, to have communion with Christ in his benefits; which longings, as they express them, seem evidently to be of such a nature as can arise from nothing but a sense of the superlative excellency of divine things, with a spiritual taste and relish of them and an esteem of them as their highest happiness and best portion. Such longing as I speak of are commonly attended with firm resolution to pursue this good for ever, together with a hoping, waiting disposition.[22]

The individual is released from her or his spiritual/psychological struggle to serve within the society.

Edwards's writings show the extent that the Puritan regular sermons had formed a narrative framework individuals indwelt. The individual's experience then confirmed the regular preaching of the Puritan divines. The biblical narrative found its plain sense in the spiritual life of the individual; the spiritual life of the individual now confirmed the truthfulness of the biblical text. The gospel became the narrative that individuals may move by faith from the despair of sin to a personal calm through the sacrificial death of Jesus, rather than the Pauline "Christ died for our sins according to the Scriptures, that he was buried, that he was raised on the third day . . . and that he appeared to . . . the Twelve" (1 Cor 15:3-5).

Soon after its composition, Edwards's *Faithful Narrative* was read by a young, zealous Anglican priest named George Whitefield. Puritan worship still focused on the reading of the Scriptures and the observance of the

---

[21]Ibid., p. 166.
[22]Ibid., p. 172.

Lord's Supper, providing a necessary ecclesial context for the regular sermon. Whitefield, however, removed the Puritan preaching narrative from
its context within the calling of believers to participate in the body and
blood of Christ and placed it within a radically different liturgical space.

Whitefield took the awakening narrative and placed it at the center of
a new rite called the awakening meeting or field preaching.[23] Such an
awakening meeting was quite simple in its form. Following the promo-
tional work of an advance man, a small group of people would gather
in a previous designated public space at a particular time. As others gathered, the small group would begin to warm up the crowd with vocal mu-
sic, usually the newly penned hymns of Isaac Watts. As the crowd
swelled, often into the thousands and occasionally even the tens of thousands, Whitefield would arrive at the scene in a carriage. Following an
extemporaneous prayer, Whitefield would commence preaching, the
central practice in the ritual. Here Whitefield performed the traditional
Puritan salvation sermon in order to bring about the awakening of sin
among those in his audience and their subsequent justification.

Yet Whitefield radically innovated and radicalized this salvation sermon as well. First, we should not underestimate the importance of moving the salvation sermon from within the gathering of the church to participate in the Lord's Supper, into the public, democratic marketplace for
all interested individuals. By this shift of location, Whitefield separated
the salvation sermon from the life of the church and its sacraments. An
individual could now be awakened and justified without any contact
with the gathering of the people of God in the Lord's Supper. The marketplace, not the church, received the Word of God as it was proclaimed.

Second, Whitefield's rhetoric differed from the Puritan's rational nar-
ration of the movement of the individual from sin to salvation. Whitefield
did not merely narrate the salvation narrative; he dramatically enacted it,
living it out on stage in his address.[24] Harry Stout aptly describes the sig-

---

[23]See Harry Stout, *The Divine Dramatist: George Whitefield and the Rise of Modern Evangelicalism* (Grand Rapids: Eerdmans, 1991).

[24]"A sarcastic account of his sermon on the New Birth printed in the Anglican *Weekly Miscellany*
called attention less to Whitefield's theme than his bodily manner: 'Hark! He talks of a Sensi-
ble New Birth—then belike he is in Labour, and the good Women around him are come to
his assistance. He dilates himself, cries out [and] is at last delivered' " (quoted in Stout, *Divine
Dramatist*, p. 40).

nificance of this shift. Earlier Puritan sermons had begun with the theological analysis of how believers become new creatures from the divine perspective through Christ's sacrifice in justification. Personal experience eventually was to catch up with what God had already done.

Whitefield's concern, however, was not the narrative of God's declaration of forgiveness. Whitefield narrated the personal experience of forgiveness for each individual. The whole focus of Whitefield's new service shifted the location of salvation from God's action in Christ to the personal experience of the individual.

Whitefield literally lived out the pangs of awakening and justification as he preached. He thereby vicariously invited others into the experience. As Stout states, Whitefield did not care about theology at all. "Instead of doctrine, he explored the feelings of New Birth and through his exploration invited hearers to experience it for themselves."[25] Whitefield moved the traditional Puritan salvation sermon deeper into the private interior of the individual.

Such a hermeneutical stance moved the already eclipsed biblical narrative farther away from the story of the people of God within creation to a place buried within the subjectivity of the individual. The Scriptural narrative now was read to encode the experience of the believer. The way was opened for the democratization of American Christianity.[26]

For preachers the plain sense of Scripture became the justifying experience of the individual as she or he moved from the anguish of sin to the delight of justification. Preaching was to translate this scriptural meaning into the life of the individual. The awakening service soon became normative for all gatherings of the church. Preachers faced the demand to read the Scriptures in order to fuse the horizon of the biblical text with the inner experience of each individual person gathered within public space of the awakening event.[27] The translation of the Scripture into the private life of the individual became the governing narrative for the interpretation of the biblical text.

---

[25]Stout, *Divine Dramatist*, pp. 38-39.

[26]See Nathan Hatch, *The Democratization of American Christianity* (New Haven, Conn.: Yale University Press, 1989).

[27]For the classical discussion of technically engineering awakening see Charles Finney, *The Lectures on Revival of Religion* (London: Banner of Truth, 1959).

This story of individual salvation, however, was not the only "biblical" narrative told within the European North American setting that originated with the Puritans. The Puritans were deeply committed to the biblical text. Even a cursory reading of the Scriptures reveals the significance of a people, Israel, throughout the Scriptures. In order to incorporate the biblical character of Israel into their lives, the Puritans also practiced "occasional sermons." Preachers proclaimed the Scriptures on special days of fasting and thanksgiving, and annual days like election day.[28] Here the biblical text was not read for the salvation of the individual but for the prosperity of the society, that is, Israel. The biblical narrative was not only collapsed into the narrative of the individual, it was redirected as well to detail the life of the newly emerging nation.

These occasional sermons arose out of the Puritan's federal covenant. The Puritans believed that God did not enter only into covenant with individuals in the covenant of grace; God also entered into covenant with a select nation. God sustained this covenant on a different basis from the covenant of grace. In the federal covenant God would uphold God's elect nation "by his providential might if they would acknowledge no other sovereign and observe the terms of obedience contained in his Word."[29] The Puritans understood New England and, soon thereafter, "America" to be this elect nation, the new Israel.

The federal covenant told a story about how God elected a nation to witness to God's righteousness through obedience to God's commandments. This nation was subject to God's special care, in terms of both reward and punishment. The federal covenant possessed a fundamentally different narrative structure from the covenant of grace. It was social and communal, but the covenant of grace was individual. The federal covenant progressed through works of righteousness; the covenant of grace solely by grace. Present-day prosperity was the goal of the federal covenant; eternal life in heaven provided the telos for the covenant of grace. The covenant of grace arose out of the New Testament and then typed "Israel" of the Old Testament to plot the spiritual progress of the individual; the federal covenant found the Old Testament's Israel in a

---

[28]For a brief introduction, see Stout, *New England Soul*, pp. 27-31.
[29]Ibid., p. 7

certain geographical area, newly "founded" by Europeans, that they soon called "America."

The Puritan divines developed their own distinct genre of sermon to proclaim the federal covenant: the jeremiad, named after the judgment-to-salvation preaching of the biblical prophet. The Canadian scholar Sacvan Bercovitch has studied the rhetoric, development, and cultural significance of these sermons in a series of significant studies.[30] Bercovitch argues that the New England Puritans transformed the jeremiad from its European predecessors and therefore set a process in motion that described the United States as God's elect nation. Such sermons called for the moral renewal of the nation in order to fulfill its divinely mandated mission and ensure its material prosperity.

According to Bercovitch, the "American jeremiad" followed a fairly fixed form.[31] The jeremiad would begin with a statement of God's standards for the righteous behavior of the elect nation on the basis of the Scriptures. The preacher would then condemn the society for the violation of these divine norms, with a subsequent threat of divine judgment. The jeremiad would end optimistically, proclaiming that divine promises of national prosperity would come if the people would mend their ways to bring the society in line with the divine plan. The form sought to unite and motivate the society to progress both morally and materially. As Berkovitch writes:

> Anxiety was one result of the ritual, its day-by-day aspect. The other aspect, equally crucial to the concept of errand, was direction and purpose. Together, these two elements define the ritual import of the jeremiad: to sustain process by imposing control, and to justify control by presenting a certain form of process as the only road to the future kingdom.[32]

While the structure and function of the jeremiad remained relatively stable across time, Berkovitch documents a significant shift that occurred in the Puritan's concept of nation. The Puritans arrived on the North American continent on a mission. They believed that they were the authentic heirs of the Reformation and the heirs of a divine national elec-

---

[30] See Sacvan Bercovitch, *The American Jeremiad* (Madison: University of Wisconsin Press, 1978).

[31] Ibid., p. 16.

[32] Ibid., p. 24.

tion that had been lost by the Stuart kings of England. They held the deep conviction that they were distinct from the rest of humanity in their election as a band of saints, an elect nation, a new Israel in covenant with God. They understood their mission to establish a church-state to bring about God's millennial reign. As a nation, the colony was out to complete God's redemption in history.[33]

Yet the Puritans' understanding of the nation soon shifted from the covenanted band of saints, the church, to people of European descent within a specific geographical region called New England. Increase Mather, in the jeremiad "The Day of Trouble Is Near" writes:

> The dealings of God with our Nation and with the Nations of the World is very different: for other Nations may sin and do wickedly and God doth not punish them, until they have filled up the Measure of their sins, and then he utterly destroyeth them; but if our Nation forsake the God of their Fathers never so little God presently cometh up on us with one Judgement or other, that so he may prevent our destruction. So [with other places] it may be that he'll reckon with them once for all at last; but if *New England* shall forsake the Lord, Judgement shall quickly overtake us, because God is not willing to destroy us.[34]

New England now was the recipient of the federal covenant, God's elect, the new Israel. While Israel was not completely de-ecclesialized, it was no longer coterminous with the church. Indeed, the concept "nation" kept expanding from its ecclesial origins. As Berkovitch states, "According to second- and third-generation orthodoxy, the New World at large—not just New England but the entire continent—was destined for an errand in sacred history. Like Canaan of old, America was the child of prophecy and promise."[35]

As the Puritans moved into the eighteenth century, their goal of a theocracy, a holy commonwealth, moved farther and farther from reality. Yet the jeremiads did not abandon the concept of the elect nation. Instead, they extended the concept to embrace America. Berkovitch again summarizes the transition:

---

[33]See Nathan Hatch, *The Sacred Cause of Liberty: Republican Thought and the Millennium in Revolutionary New England* (New Haven, Conn.: Yale University Press, 1977).
[34]Increase Mather, quoted in Bercovitch, *American Jeremiad*, p. 60.
[35]Bercovitch, *American Jeremiad*, p. 69.

Intent on preserving the past, they [the eighteenth-century Puritan preachers] transformed it (as legend) into a malleable guide to the future. Seeking to defend the Good Old Way, they abstracted from its antiquated social forms the larger, vaguer, and more flexible forms of symbol and metaphor *(new chosen people, city on a hill, promised land, destined progress, New Eden, American Jerusalem),* and so facilitated the movement from visible saint to American patriot, sacred errand to manifest destiny, colony to republic to imperial power. In spite of themselves, as it were, the latter-day orthodoxy freed their rhetoric for the use and abuse of subsequent generations of Americans.[36]

As the American Revolution broke out, the jeremiad essentially transformed the emerging United States into the new Israel. In the Revolution the preachers "connected religion and patriotism, and in their sermons and prayers represented the cause of America as the cause of Heaven."[37]

The colonies, soon to be the United States of America, had displaced the church as the elect people of God, the heirs of promises to Abraham and a central character within the biblical story. Not only had the Puritans collapsed biblical narrative into the life of the individual, they also had substantially de-ecclesialized it. The North American Protestant environment had emptied the church of its place in the biblical narrative as the people of God. The Scriptures were understood to narrate the individual's pursuit of salvation and America's divinely elect mission for prosperity, assuming, of course, that it maintained a biblically based righteousness.

This is not to say that the church was explained out of existence; it was not. Instead, the church, like God, was subordinated within the primary theological narratives of the individual and the emerging nation to a role as a supporting actor. Within the North American Protestant context, the church did not exist, as in the biblical narrative, as a communal witness to the new creation gathered from all nations through the death and resurrection of Jesus. The church existed instead as a mediating, voluntary organization to call individuals as individuals to eternal bliss and to guard the moral mission of America in order to protect its prosperity and divinely sanctioned mission. The eclipse of biblical narrative was

[36]Ibid., p. 92.
[37]Ibid., p. 122.

also the eclipse of the direct theological significance of the church's witness in the world.

We have not pursued this historical analysis out of disinterested academic or antiquarian interest. It is part of a theological argument for why it is necessary, given the contemporary North American cultural environment, to adopt a tragic hermeneutical moment in order to weave a local congregation's life into the biblical narrative, the story of God. As the biblical narrative dissolved in the face of the transitions of modernity, the Puritans renarrated biblical language and imagery into the covenant of grace and the federal covenant. These dual narratives have long outlived their origins in the New England holy commonwealth. Today they form the narrative horizons that shape the lives of many, if not most, within American culture, especially in its Christian or religious communities.

To this day the narrative structures of the covenant of grace and the federal covenant form a common underlying narrative for American Christianity in its evangelical and mainline embodiments. In North America the narrative of salvation entails the movement of an individual from an unpleasant state to a state of genuine happiness. These states might be defined with different terms, but the underlying narrative structure remains the same. For conservatives, an individual may move from sin and guilt to eternal life through forgiveness offered by Christ's substitutionary death. For liberals, an individual may move from alienation to authentic human existence and to exercise fully their human rights through the Christ. The covenant of grace, the movement from sin to salvation to service, underlies both; only the definitions of these states change.

Likewise, the federal covenant persists in defining the church's political witness in the world. Within the larger culture it is assumed that the church exists to serve the American society as its moral guardian in order to insure America's prosperity and mission in the world. The church's own polity, based on forgiveness and reconciliation, becomes secondary. The church might influence individual Christians as a valid interest group to help ensure the justice of the American state. Yet difficulties immediately arise again, for justice is defined within the contours of the American state in either a conservative or liberal form. The stridency of the division within the North American church according to the contours of the right-left split of the contemporary culture wars certainly witnesses to this. Yet both sides assume the fundamental basis of the federal covenant: the church exists to form a righteous nation so that this elect nation can prosper materially and fulfill its democratic mission within the world.

If this is so, American Christian culture has been remarkable uniform and conservative in its underlying narrative horizons throughout the past two and a half centuries. This observation would not surprise Bercovitch or other observers of American Christianity. From its Puritan origins, Bercovitch finds

> a ritual leveling of all sects within the framework of *American* religion. *By their very contradictions they were made to correspond.* . . . The result was a Babel of religious doctrines, united by their common reverence for "the American enterprise and [a] common conviction of its millennial denouement." As Tocqueville shrewdly observed, "Each sect worships God in its own fashion, but all preach the same morality in the name of God." Americans "practice religion out of self-interest," but "religion prevents them from imagining and forbids them to dare" anything that might basically challenge the "public order."[38]

Underneath the cacophony of supposed pluralism lies fundamental narrative structures that demand uniformity—and thereby conformity.

To adopt a comedic hermeneutic in preaching would be to continue to translate the biblical text into either—or both—of the Puritan narratives, and thus to contribute to the continued eclipse of biblical narrative. If the above arguments hold, this can no longer be done naively nor innocently. Such a strategy must be seen as the conscious attempt to suppress biblical narrative, separate it from its proper social location in the life of the church, and marginalize the church by placing it as a secondary loyalty in relationship to American culture.

I believe that this analysis provides in itself adequate justification for risking a tragic moment in homiletical interpretation of the Scriptures. Yet I would like to push the argument one additional step. I believe that to pursue a comedic homiletic in the contemporary cultural environment, even for the temporary entrepreneurial success of the church within the culture, endangers the long-term viability of the church. To

---

[38]Ibid.

eclipse the biblical narrative by the narratives of the individual or nation supplants the church in favor of individual self-interest and the preservation of the public order. Over time, such a move has—and promises to continue to—undercut the viability of sustaining the life of concrete congregations. In other words, to eclipse biblical narrative is also to eclipse the concrete life of the church over time.

"Church" and "Sect" and the Rise and Fall of Christian Movements in America

Through the influence of the Puritans, two narratives emerged to supplant the biblical narrative in American Christianity, a narrative of the individual moving from sin to salvation to service and a narrative of God responding with prosperity to God's elect nation according to their righteousness. These two narratives were nurtured and disseminated in dual preaching settings: (1) the covenant of grace in Sunday worship and the newly crafted awakening meeting, and (2) the federal covenant in fasting and thanksgiving services, along with set special events such as election-day addresses. These dual settings allowed the Puritans, for a time, to maintain simultaneously the dual narratives of the covenant of grace and the federal covenant to strike a balance between parallel narratives of individual and national upward mobility.

As time went on, however, the New England theocratic social setting that allowed the consistent performance of both regular and occasional sermons faded away. Preachers lost the opportunity to maintain both covenantal discourses in different settings. Instead, preachers had to choose which narrative was most significant for their congregation when they gathered. Should they preach the salvation sermon or the jeremiad? Dynamics embedded in the two genres of sermons made it difficult in practice to maintain such parallel emphases. Congregations, even denominations, became defined more and more by preaching either the covenant of grace or the federal covenant.

Such historical circumstances have deeply affected the life of the church in North America. By giving up the biblical narrative, the church simultaneously gave up its own particular sociological commitments as the church. As a secondary social-political grouping, the church became part of civil society and thus surrendered to other sociological-political forces. One can see the implications of this surrender in the historical life of the church. The eclipse of biblical narrative, with the loss of the theological centrality of the church, has set in motion a cycle of church growth and decline within the North American culture. Roger Finke and Rodney Stark in *The Churching of America 1776-1990* have documented this cycle that seems to continue to this day with the decline in mainline denominations and the rise of third-wave movements such as Calvary Chapel and the Vineyard Fellowship.

Finke and Starke assembled church membership statistics from the United States from the Revolutionary War onward according to denominational adherence. Not only did they gather absolute numbers of church members; they compared the percentage of adherence to the total population as well as the percentage of market share that specific denominations maintained of the churched populations. What Finke and Starke discovered was "the churching of America":

> On the eve of the Revolution only about 17 percent of Americans were churched. By the start of the Civil War this proportion had rise [sic] dramatically, to 37 percent. The immense dislocation of the war caused a serious decline in adherence in the South, which is reflected in the overall decline of 35 percent in the 1870 census. The rate then began to rise once more, and by 1906 slightly more than half of the U.S. population was churched. Adherence rates reached 56 percent by 1926. Since then the rate has been rather stable although inching upwards. By 1980 church adherence was about 62 percent.[39]

The church in the United States has progressively grown in numbers of members from its inception—perhaps a surprise for Christians shaped by the traditional rhetoric of the jeremiad with its language of moral crisis and decline.

Finke and Starke have documented, however, that growth has not been distributed evenly within all Christian groups. The life of the church in the United States has been anything but stable. What they discovered instead were cycles of accelerated growth of specific groups that led to a plateau of membership before a decline of the market share

---

[39]Roger Finke and Rodney Starke, *The Churching of America 1776-1990: Winners and Losers in Our Religious Economy* (New Brunswick, N.J.: Rutgers University Press, 1992), p. 15.

of membership set in. Late in the eighteenth century the Methodists and
the Baptists had meteoric rises of membership as the Congregationalists
and Episcopalians faced declines. From the middle of the nineteenth
century on, however, the Methodist Episcopal Church stabilized and
then declined in its relative percentage of members, displaced by Roman
Catholics, Southern Baptists, and Holiness Churches. In the past fifty
years mainline denominations have fought a losing battle to hold on to
membership while Assemblies of God churches have flourished. As
Finke and Starke aptly conclude, "the mainline bodies are always
headed for the sideline."[40]

Finke and Starke are not content to provide a statistical analysis of
rates of church membership in the United States. They openly state that
they do not merely want to describe the statistics; they want to explain
them.[41] Here Finke and Starke draw upon the thought of Max Weber,
Ernst Troeltsch and H. Richard Niebuhr. As a result they openly place
their study within a capitalist economic model that it always had presupposed.[42]

Finke and Starke argue that the needs of individuals for different
types of religious organizations provide the key to the growth and decline of religious firms in America. Sects attract individuals who need
a "strict and otherworldly faith"; churches serve the "segment of the
market" with less need of strictness or otherworldliness. According to
Finke and Starke, sects have the potential to generate more significant
commitment from their members. They are therefore able to generate
more volunteer labor and capital necessary to compete for new members in the "unregulated religious marketplace" provided by the dis-
establishment of "religion" in the United States.[43]

---

[40]Ibid., p. 275.

[41]Ibid., p. 21.

[42]Their presupposition on the "naturalness" of capitalistic market processes belies the historical
contingency and powers that produced such dynamics. See Milbank, *Theology and Social
Theory*.

[43]Again, Finke and Starke naively claim that this market is "unregulated." There is careful reg-
ulation of "religion" in the United States to keep it private and voluntary—that is, to keep it
so that it does not challenge the authority of the contemporary liberal nation-state to regulate
the bodies of persons who live in their geographic regions of control by assigning it to a "private" versus a "public" realm. As Slavoj Zizek writes, "One possible definition of modernity
is: the social order in which religion is no longer integrated into and identified with a particular cultural life-form, but acquires autonomy, so that it can survive as the same religion in

Yet over time sects tend to become churches: "when their tension
with the surrounding culture is greatly reduced, they soon cease to grow
and eventually begin to decline."[44] The churches are no longer able to
generate the commitment necessary to provide the capital, human and
otherwise, to compete in the marketplace. When the church is no different from the neighborhood watch group in ethos or mission or consequences, it is much easier for a family to stay in bed to watch the neighborhood over the paper before the NFL games begin than to load the
kids in the car to attend worship services at a small church, for which
they provide the financial backing.

Finke and Starke write as if they have removed themselves from their
own concrete historical situation to reduce the life of congregations to
some previous, more basic, objective category of sociology. They therefore remove the growth and decline of churches in the United States
from the particular historical and political horizons in North America, except for a free-market religious economics. Finke and Starke thereby reduce the church to a merely social rather than a theological reality. Here
they fall prey to the deeper, anti-ecclesial commitments of the field of
the sociology of religion.[45] Christians must seriously question the underlying commitments of such an interpretative scheme. As Phil Kenneson
writes, "By creating an ostensibly autonomous realm called 'the social,'
sociology claims to explain what is *really* going on in the world without
recourse to theological interpretations."[46]

The naiveté of Finke and Starke's approach becomes evident in the
contradictions between the data that they gather and their definitions of
church and sect. For Finke and Starke the categories of church and sect
are forms of religious organizations that are "the end points of a contin-
uum made up of the degree of tension between religious organizations
and their sociocultural environments. . . . *Churches* are religious bodies

---

different cultures. . . . [T]he price to be paid is that religion is reduced to a secondary epiphe-
nomenon with regard to the secular functioning of the social totality" (Slavoj Zizek, *The Pup-
pet and the Dwarf: The Perverse Core of Christianity* [Cambridge, Mass.: MIT Press, 2003], p.
3; cf. also Talal Asad, "The Limits of Religious Criticism in the Middle East: Notes on Islamic
Public Argument," in *Genealogies of Religion*, pp. 201-8).

[44]Finke and Starke, *Churching of America*, p. 148.

[45]See Milbank, *Theology and Social Theory*; see also Philip D. Kenneson, *Beyond Sectarianism:
Re-imagining Church and World* (Valley Forge, Penn.: Trinity Press International, 1999).

[46]Kenneson, *Beyond Sectarianism*, p. 60.

in a relatively low state of tension with their environments. *Sects* are religious bodies in a relatively high state of tension with their environments."[47] Yet the examples of growing groups actually contradict the nontheological, abstract social categories that they give.

For instance, Finke and Starke rightfully draw attention to the importance of George Whitefield, the Anglo-American revivalist, the early churching of America and a shift of adherence from Puritan Congregationalists to Baptist congregations. Whitefield, however, did not stand in tension with the American culture but articulated its deepest convictions. Whitefield liturgically eclipsed the biblical narrative in his awakening meetings that reduced all of Christianity to the individualistic covenant of grace. Such individualizing and de-ecclesializing of Christianity deeply accommodated the faith given to the saints to the democratic convictions necessary to bring about the American rebellion against England. Mark Noll tells a fascinating story in his *A History of Christianity in the United States and Canada*. It is worth quoting Noll's own words in full:

> In 1775, colonial troops were mustered near Newburyport, Massachusetts, in preparation for an expedition to Canada. The hope was that a show of force to the north would draw Canadians into the struggle for independence from Britain. Before the troops set out, however, they paused for a sermon from a young chaplain, the Reverend Samuel Spring. After the message, Spring and some of the officers visited a nearby crypt. It was the tomb of George Whitefield, who had died in Newburyport only five years earlier. Together the minister and officers pried open the coffin and removed the clerical and wrist bands from the revivalist's skeleton. Somehow it was thought that the spirit of America's greatest preacher of spiritual freedom would assist them in this struggle for political freedom.[48]

The subsequent growth of Christianity arose from Whitefield's willingness to de-ecclesialize the faith by proclaiming an extreme subjective form of the covenant of grace in accommodation to the emerging political context of the United States. Seen from this perspective it is no wonder Whitefield evoked such admiration from his deist friend Ben Franklin—they ultimately shared the most profound convictions about

---

[47]Finke and Starke, *Churching of America*, pp. 40-41.
[48]Mark Noll, *A History of the United States in the United States and Canada* (Grand Rapids: Eerdmans, 1992), p. 113.

individual autonomy. Franklin merely overlaid his convictions with deist language; Whitefield with Christian language.

What Finke and Starke call upstart sects were actually intuitively accommodating to the convictions of the environment of the new United States. Such a reading corresponds precisely with the results of Nathan Hatch's marvelous study *The Democratization of American Christianity*. Hatch argues that the "process of Christianization within American popular culture" occurred through the "democratization of Christianity," having "less to do with specifics of polity and governance and more with the incarnation of the church into popular culture.[49] From the perspective of wealth, established social power and the academy, such movement might have looked sectarian. From the perspective of Jeffersonian democracy these groups articulated the deepest convictions of their environment through the persistent proclamation of the covenant of grace. Finke and Starke's data does not describe sectarian movements, even in their own definition. Rather they describe the institutional success of those who, through the covenant of grace, provided—and still provide—Christian legitimation for Christian individuals who may understand their lives and allegiances primarily as members of a democratic society rather than as participants in the body of Christ, the church.

If this is so, Finke and Starke's statistics emerge from the historical horizons of an American Christianity that has lost the biblical narrative and become de-ecclesialized. From a theological perspective the cycle of growth and decline witnesses to God's judgment for the eclipse of biblical narrative and the loss of the theological centrality of the church. When the church is turned from being "a holy nation, a kingdom of priests" into a mediating institution to support an agenda for individuals or nations, God will not allow such a church to sustain its witness across time.

We may become even more precise in our interpretation. The covenant of grace presupposed a particular Christian language. Even if the covenant of grace restructured the biblical narrative and was powered by an intense personal experience, it drew its Christian legitimacy and uniqueness from its particularly biblical language. As such the salvation covenant presupposes—and requires—an ecclesial formation, both to

---

[49]Hatch, *Democratization of American Christianity*, p. 9.

maintain the biblical language and shape and interpret the experience. In other words, while the covenant of grace does not itself produce persons for ecclesial formation, it is parasitical upon it. The covenant of grace presupposes a functional ecclesiology, even if it cannot sustain it over time.

What seems to happen is a process of what Donald Dayton has called "embourgoisement."[50] With no ecclesiology committed to the gospel teachings of Jesus or the Pauline or Jamesian ecclesial formation, the covenant of grace, which often begins embracing the poor, tends to become upwardly mobile. Because salvation is solely individual, the church moves toward the wealthy and powerful within society as the preferred market for the individual narrative of salvation. By reaching the influential, it is hoped that covenant of grace will envelop more and more people through the resources and influence that power and wealth possess. Such a move requires that we leave a specific market niche to a broader, more general demographic market.

The narrative structure of the covenant of grace provides such an opportunity. The preacher can adjust the terms of the same narrative structure to fit the perceived needs of a broader, wider more affluent social group. More relevant therapeutic language can easily replace the more traditional language of sin and salvation. Preachers can easily transform the terms of the covenant of grace. An individual's trip from this world to heaven has the identical structure as an individual's therapeutic journey of finding his or her own self-fulfillment in Jesus to cope with stresses that arise from full participation in and commitments to the structures of American life.

Within the church one experiences this shift of the language of the narrative in a therapeutic transformation of gospel; outside the church it is even more evident. Individual spirituality centered in subjective experience replaces the faithful life pursued within the context of an ecclesial community. Pastors must more and more attempt to address a setting in which adherents seek their own personal well-being in order to generate the commitment necessary to keep a concrete congregation functioning

---

[50]Donald W. Dayton, " 'The Search for the Historical Evangelicalism'; George Marsden's History of Fuller Seminary as a Case Study," *Christian Scholars Review* 23, no. 1 (1993): 12-33, esp. p. 32.

in even a minimal way. In the process the church looks less and less distinct and more and more like the rich and famous within the society.

Yet another narrative transformation occurs as well. As the church engages those influential within the culture with the covenant of grace, the tendency is to switch the emphasis of preaching to the federal covenant. Having the influential and the powerful in the church, the preacher seeks to provide the moral guidance, in general terms, for the society at large. The church still remains a mediating institution. But whereas the covenant of grace requires a functional ecclesiology to form people into the appropriate experience within the church, the federal covenant renders the church completely unnecessary except as a forum for moral judgment. The nation, not the church, is God's elect. One need only participate righteously in the society to be part of God's people. Direct social activism or the authentic embodiment of a person's own values will often be more effective than "wasting time" being members of the church. Seeking to serve the society rather than God, the church has no sense of alienation from the principalities and powers. The church loses the ability to generate the particular, embodied faithful lives necessary to maintain the life of the people of God in the world.

Finke and Starke, therefore, are right about mainline congregations not being able to generate commitment to sustain their Christian witness across time, let alone to evangelize. Yet this is not anchored in an ahistorical social process of market economics. It is anchored in the loss of a biblical ecclesiology, itself found in the eclipse of the biblical narrative. The sect-church cycle analyzed by Finke and Starke represents two different forms of an already accommodated Christianity. One, the so-called sect, however, requires practically some form of ecclesial existence and discipline. Here, at least the Scriptures are read and some form of communal Christian virtues and practices are required, even if the ultimate end of the story is within the individual, not the redemption of all creation.

A church formed by a nationalized federal covenant, however, does not require a people whose allegiances separate the church from the world. The nation is the elect, not the church. An individual might as well just devote him- or herself directly to the prosperity of the nation in activism. With no witness or specifically Christian virtues required to sustain the life of such a people, God's judgment comes, and the church is met with precipitous decline. Congregations shaped by the federal covenant move from the mainline to the sideline because they have abandoned the distinctive witness of the church. Join the Jaycees; it's cheaper.

The cycle of growth and decline documented by Finke and Starke comes from the accommodation of the church to its environment in the United States and is not a natural part of living as the people of God in the world. This is not to say that living in the church as a peculiar people, characters within God's story of the new creation, will lead to massive social renewal. My guess is that it would more likely provoke opposition as the church refuses to let itself be defined by the economics of consumerism and the militarism of nationalism. Even more, some of the most voracious opposition will most likely come from other Christians. Such phenomena give witness to the deep shaping of a culture itself shaped by the jeremiad that believes that the nation, not the church in every tribe and nation, is God's new Israel.

Even if such a theological witness would not bring about the third "great awakening," I think that the formation of specific congregations into a peculiar people would stop the cycle of ecclesial ups and downs over time in American society, and provide for the long-term witness of the church. Rather than large numbers in highly visible places joining the church, it is more likely that such congregations' witness will expand imperceptibly, like the workings of leaven and salt, like the growth of first- and second-century Christianity. Such congregations will maintain their witness across time because of the faithfulness of their practices found in an intentional commitment to forming and being formed as a peculiar people living in the world as a sign of God's love for all creation.

While the covenant of grace and the federal covenant eclipsed the biblical narrative, the Scriptures still remain to call forth a faithful people through the workings of the Spirit. In the practices of such a people, the biblical narrative may emerge from the shadows to sustain and guide and nurture congregations in their witness. Congregations who embark on such an adventure can embrace the biblical narrative's mission to live as a sign of God's redemption in the world. This community will be a visible reminder that the redemption that God the Father has wrought through the Son by the power of the Spirit has also been offered to the whole world—if they would repent and be baptized and live faithfully as the people of the God, members of the church. This church would be defined by Jesus' faithfulness to God in the world, faithfulness seen ultimately on the cross. It would understand that conversion is more than a personal experience of a personal relationship with God; conversion requires the incorporation of an individual into a new people, a new family and developing the necessary virtues to live as aliens and exiles in this new transnational community. Such a congregation will live by the Word proclaimed that redirects and re-forms the lives of those who would live faithfully as the people of God in the world.

Conclusion

We have traveled far in these first two chapters. Chapter two has attempted to map, in broad terms, the historical horizons of American Christianity. At first sight this historical-cultural criticism might seem far from the concerns of chapter one. But it is not. First, the theological formation of congregations, indeed the cultural formation of a large segment of American culture, has been shaped or at least reinforced by preaching. Puritan divines and revivalist preachers were not secondary theologians but the very shapers of the theological formation of many believers and congregations in American history.

Yet we have discovered that preachers in North America have refused a genuine tragic moment in the proclamation of the Word. Preachers' participation in the eclipse of biblical narrative has turned the church into a service organization, a particular type of a larger type of organizations called "communities of faith." Within the narrative horizons provided by North American culture, the church exists for the salvation of the individual and the moral formation of the nation, but has no inherent theological significance itself.

Preaching between these covenants has set into motion movements of growth followed by the embourgoisement and then the decline of the church in North America. Attempts to manage such dynamics by church officials for the growth of the church are ultimately doomed to failure. They presuppose the naturalness of the problem, working consistently to treat symptoms while the disease presses on.

Underneath the story I have told, however, is a hopeful appeal. Given the eclipse of the biblical narrative and the ensuing social consequences for the church, this story argues that somehow we must embrace a tragic moment in contemporary homiletics that opens up the possibility of re-formation of local congregations. "Bible-believing" congregations, formed by the cultural horizons of American Christianity, have heard and read the Christian Scriptures as individuals and citizens of the United States rather than as members of the church catholic. Faced with these cultural and congregational expectations, preachers try to use the come-dic fusion of the biblical text into these horizons. They hope, therefore, to maintain the adherence of their present members and prove the rele-vance of the Bible to seekers who may visit their worship services. Iron-ically, in the process they provide biblical sanction for the deepest con-victions of the society rather than weaving congregations into God's story, forming them into a kingdom of priests, a holy nation.

In such a setting, the in-breaking of the gospel must embrace a tragic moment, reading the Scriptures against the world for the sake of the world. Ironically, pastors must learn to preach against the culture in or-der to interpret the Scriptures for their congregations in a way that makes their own gathering as the church significant. We may discover the ulti-mate relevance in our preaching by becoming appropriately irrelevant! Preachers must be willing to take their congregations into the abyss where the Holy Spirit, speaking through the biblical texts, challenges our deepest convictions about the Christian life.

How? I am sure that there are multiple ways. Yet at the very least, such a homiletic involves renarrating individual and communal lives as char-acters within the biblical narrative. In chapter three I will offer one dis-tinct homiletical rhetoric to weave congregations from the covenant of grace and the federal covenant, or even plain secularity, into the biblical narrative's calling together of a people of God through the faithfulness of Jesus as a witness to God's reconciling love in a fallen, unjust world. In other words, I will offer a distinct rhetoric for the homiletical forma-tion of the church as a peculiar people through weaving the story of God. It is to this practical task that we must now turn.

3

WEAVING THE STORY

The Biblical Narrative and a
Homiletic Rhetoric of Turning

Rock climbing is a popular leisure activity in western North America. The activity takes an enormous amount of technical knowledge, equipment, training and skill—not to mention a basic disregard for heights! And rock climbing is much different than ascending a ladder. It involves ropes, bolts, carabiners and anchors. Unlike trapeze artists, safety nets are not part of the apparatus. Climbers have to find the best way up a cliff whose surfaces are uneven and jagged with overhangs and fissures. Ropes secured between the climbers and anchors in the rock itself provide the protection as they move up the face of the rock.

Usually, climbers cannot proceed vertically up the rock. Though supported by ropes, foot- and handholds occur to the left or right, and climbers must go where the holds are. When they get far enough off the ground or away from the last anchor, they drive an anchor into the rock, and clip the support rope into it. In this way they ascend safely and consistently toward the summit.

Sometimes, however, a major obstacle looms in the climber's path. At this point, he or she will drive an anchor firmly into the rock and then turn immediately right or left, moving horizontally for a distance until the overhang or obstacle is cleared. A new anchor provides security to close the horizontal move. Then the upward ascent can continue. Having met the obstacle, the climber does not force his or her way over it or through it; rather the climber negotiates the obstacle by acknowledging it and then moving around it. Movement grounded in anchors, knowing when to turn to circumvent obstacles and when to ascend toward the summit, marks the expertise of a good rock climber.

I would like to suggest a rhetoric of preaching that looks much like rock climbing.[1] The loss of the church's theological significance presents a massive obstacle in preaching faithfully. If today's church is the victim of the eclipse of the biblical narrative, we might find a key to retrieving the biblical narrative in the formation of the people of God. In other words, one crucial dimension of recovering the biblical narrative is rediscovering the significance of the congregation as the visible body of Christ in the world. Such a congregation would not live as a voluntary service agency dispensing individual salvation while divided by national boundaries, but as "a chosen people, a royal priesthood, a holy nation, a people belonging to God, that you may declare the praises of him who called you out of darkness into his wonderful light" (1 Pet 2:9).

Our situation presents a large, tragic obstacle for the preacher. Our context calls for embracing a tragic hermeneutical moment in preaching, which is necessary in order to turn a congregation from the narrative frameworks provided by North American culture so they can live as characters within the biblical narrative. Acknowledging contextual obstacles and turning the congregation from the cultural presuppositions into the biblical text becomes paramount for faithful preaching. Having turned a congregation homiletically, the Spirit can form a congregation within the biblical narrative as a peculiar people with a distinctive, sustainable Christian witness. Preaching then seeks to empower the congregation to live within God's story of the redemption of all creation so that human lives might reflect God's glory for the sake of the world.

Nonbiblical narratives have profoundly formed North American congregations, often in the name of the Bible. Renarrating a congregation's life calls for disruption, even tragedy, an acknowledgment that our way up is blocked. The tragic moment is not pleasant—it calls for a rupture, an "overhang" that blocks the text and the hearer. It demands that a

---

[1]Thanks to Rev. Rodney Bertholet, pastor of Southeast Community Church of the Nazarene in Portland, Oregon, for giving me this helpful analogy in a master's of ministry class I taught, "The Old Testament in the Christian Pulpit," San Diego, California, in January 2004.

preacher say, We cannot pass that way to get to the end of our journey. Preachers must find ways around obstacles to hearing the text from within the biblical story. How do we do this without losing our congregation?

Such a task calls for careful pastoral reflection. In its very practice, preaching must communicate. Homiletics presupposes shared convictions between the text and the congregation that provide the conditions for the communication of the Word of God. But how do we unearth fundamental narrative convictions that prohibit congregations from hearing the Word of God? Given the interpretive horizons of American Christianity, is it possible for pastors to preach so that the congregation might have ears to hear?

This chapter extols a rhetoric of turning. *Turning,* of course, is an English translation for the Hebrew word, *šub,* or "repentance." A homiletic of turning, or repentance, seeks to turn a congregation from one narrative world into another, to renarrate the world at the deepest convictional level of a congregation, moving them from narratives of the individual and the nation into the narrative of the people of God through Jesus Christ by the power of the Spirit. Before exploring homiletics as a means of repentance, I first will provide a brief theological summary of the biblical narrative, highlighting the centrality of the church as the "place" in which Christians must stand in order to hear the biblical narrative.

The Centrality of the Church Within the Biblical Narrative

Christian Scriptures form a narrative, a story. On one level, this is readily apparent, based on the simple observation that the Christian Scriptures begin with the book of Genesis and end with the book of Revelation. The "heavens and earth" (Gen 1:1) that God creates in the beginning is transformed into the "new heaven and new earth" (Rev 21:1), and the tree of life from Genesis 2 reappears "for the healing of the nations" in Revelation 22.

Even as some have reclaimed the narrative structure of the Scriptures, others have contested this claim based on the complexity of the biblical narrative and other types of literature found within the Scriptures. Without denying either the narrative complexity or different genres within the Scriptures, such objections do not adequately grasp the nature of narratives. Narratives work at different levels. Any good story will have multiple story lines that branch off from the main plot, often, but not always, to return. Narratives are consistently filled with nonnarrative material, but such material falls within—and must be interpreted within— the framework, the deep structure, of the broader story.[2]

Similarly, the Scriptures present a narrative deep structure, a five-act drama of salvation that unifies the whole as one grand story, God's story.[3] I will briefly summarize the main events of the story. The narrative begins with God's creation of all that is good, with humanity, male and female, simultaneously created in the image of God. Yet God's good creation turns away from God as human disobedience brings havoc, violence and strife into God's creation. The second act of the drama begins with God's election of Abraham to bring forth a people as a blessing to the nations (Gen 12:1-4). God brings forth the children of Israel from Abraham and Sarah. God redeems Israel from slavery in Egypt and calls them to be a kingdom of priests and a holy nation by giving them the law at Sinai (Ex 19—20). Ultimately, God faithfully gives Israel the Promised Land and eventually promises David that his dynasty will rule over Israel forever (2 Sam 7). When Israel wanders from obedience to God and fails in their care of each other, especially the poor and the vulnerable, the Word of God comes through the prophets to call Israel back to faithfulness to their mission to be God's people through mutual care. God even grants Israel wisdom so that the people might live wisely in their mission amid the nations, beginning with the fear of God. The second act, the life of Israel, covers much of the Old Testament.

The third act begins as God brings forth Jesus Christ, the son of Abraham, the son of David (Mt 1:1). Four different accounts of the life of Jesus tell the same underlying story. Jesus lived, did signs and wonders,

[2]See Gerard Loughlin, *Telling God's Story: Bible, Church, and Narrative Theology* (Cambridge: Cambridge University Press, 1996), where he argues "*how* it is possible for the Bible to tell many narratives, but only one story" (p. 51) through the use of the narratological theory of Gerard Gennette (pp. 52-63).

[3]For a similar treatment of the biblical writings, but as a six-act drama, see Craig G. Bartholomew and Michael W. Goheen, *The Drama of Scripture: Finding Our Place in the Biblical Story* (Grand Rapids: Baker Academic, 2004). Whereas here we combine creation and fall into one "act," Bartholomew and Goheen speak of them as two separate acts.

taught, and gathered the people, particularly the poor, into the kingdom of God, a renewed Israel. His life, teaching and practices, however, fostered human opposition. Jesus gave himself over to death on the cross in obedient faithfulness to God the Father. This, however, was not the last word. His faithfulness was vindicated by the Father's faithfulness to him in the resurrection: "Jesus Christ of Nazareth, whom you crucified but whom God raised from the dead" (Acts 4:10).[4]

The resurrection initiates the fourth act in the drama. After the resurrection of Jesus, God the Father sends forth the Holy Spirit to call not only Jews but Gentiles into the continuing story of Israel through the life, teachings, death and resurrection of Jesus. In the life of the church God fulfills God's own promise to Abraham to make Israel a blessing to all nations through Jesus Christ. The church lives as a sign of God's faithfulness to the world, a visible sign of the resurrection of Jesus and God's coming kingdom over all creation. The church is called to live according to the faithfulness of Jesus, even in his sufferings, amid the nations, awaiting the fifth and final act of the drama: the consummation of all things in the return of Jesus. In this return God will restore all things through the Son: "The kingdom of the world has become the kingdom of our Lord and of his Christ, and he will reign for ever and ever" (Rev 11:15).

This is not the place to rehearse in depth a complete biblical theology as story.[5] For our purposes it is sufficient to emphasize that Scripture presents a story for Christians to live within as the Holy Spirit calls others into the people of God through the life, death and resurrection of Jesus. Jesus represents the central hinge event in the story, the "Righteous One" in whom God restores Israel and ultimately all creation.[6] As the hinge

---

[4]For the obedience of Jesus as providing the common motif through all for Gospels of the New Testament, see Hans Frei, *The Identity of Jesus Christ* (Eugene, Ore.: Wipf & Stock, 1997), pp. 132-83; for the importance of the faithfulness of Jesus within the apostle Paul's thought and underlying narrative see Richard B. Hays, *The Faith of Jesus Christ: The Narrative Substructure of Galatians 3:1-4:11*, 2nd ed. (Grand Rapids: Eerdmans, 2002). For Frei's influence on Hays see esp. Hays, *The Faith of Jesus Christ*, pp. xxiv-xxv.

[5]See Michael Lodahl, *The Story of God: Wesleyan Theology and Biblical Narrative* (Kansas City: Beacon Hill, 1994), for a more developed systematic approach to the Scripture as story, albeit with process theological categories looming in the background.

[6]See, classically, Oscar Cullman, *Christ and Time: The Primitive Christian Conception of Time and History*, rev. ed. (Philadelphia: Westminster Press, 1964), for Christ as the "mid-point" in the biblical conception of time.

event Jesus cannot be understood outside of the previous story line—
creation and Israel—and the story line that follows—the church and the
new creation. Jesus' significance cannot be abstracted from the particular
narrative that the Scriptures form. As the fulfillment of creation and the
story of Israel, Jesus initiates the life of the church that witnesses to the
coming new creation. The story of Jesus, the gospel, opens into the story
of the church. Moreover, just as we cannot separate his teachings from
his death and resurrection, so we cannot separate his death and resurrection from the embodiment of his teachings in the community he
founds, the church. As John Milbank writes:

> The name of Jesus is attached to a descriptive content at the point where
> the word of the gospel ceases to be mere teaching, and is made "real" and
> powerful in a new social body which can transgress every human bound-
> ary, and adopts no law in addition to that of "life," or the imperative to
> the greater strength and beauty which is attendant upon a diverse yet har-
> monious, mutually reconciled community.[7]

Within the biblical narrative the church stands as the people of God
gathered in fulfillment of God's promise to Abraham through the faithfulness of Jesus in anticipation of the coming completion of God's rule
through all creation.

To live within the biblical narrative, then, demands that we understand ourselves as occupying the narrative space between Christ's resurrection and Christ's return, between the "already" of the incarnation and
the "not yet" of Christ's return.[8] Christians stand within the biblical narrative between the life, teachings, death and resurrection of Jesus, and
the restoration of all creation. Yet Christians do not occupy this space as
autonomous individuals in the biblical narrative; humans only find their
true individuality as part of the church. The biblical narrative calls forth
the church's communal witness as a sign of what is to come over all creation. When preachers proclaim the Scriptures, it is within the particular

---

[7]John Milbank, "The Name of Jesus," in *The Word Made Strange: Theology, Language, Culture*
(Oxford: Blackwell, 1997), p. 153.
[8]Within evangelicalism G. E. Ladd eloquently spoke of this tension in his classic work, *Jesus
and the Kingdom: The Eschatology of Biblical Realism* (Waco, Tex.: Word, 1969). The book
was later published as *The Presence of the Future: The Eschatology of Biblical Realism* (Grand
Rapids: Eerdmans, 1974).

narrative space afforded to the church, a people founded by Jesus as "a new city, a new kind of human community, Israel-become-the-Church."[9] Preaching calls the church to its communal witness of the already-that-will-be.

Scriptures provide the "narrative home" for the church. The church literally lives within the biblical narrative, whether it wants to or not! This is not our decision, but God's. Once we grasp this, it becomes clear why Christians have read the biblical narrative typologically: the story of Israel amid the nations is the church's story as well. Israel foreshadows the contemporary life of the church. We read the Scriptures typologically to help the church live faithfully from within the biblical narrative. "Typology is fundamentally a Christological and ecclesial form of interpretation. . . . The movement is from events in the story of Israel through Jesus as the center and 'archetype' of the story to the church as the ongoing bearer of the story."[10] The whole notion of Scripture in the early church depended on such a spiritual exegesis.[11] Christians must read the Scriptures typologically to understand their ongoing part in the biblical narrative. As Campbell recognizes:

> Figural interpretation serves not only to unify the biblical narrative, but also to incorporate the contemporary world, particularly the contemporary people of God, into that story. . . . Through typological interpretation, the world of the contemporary people of God is seen and described in terms of the patterns and connections discerned in the biblical narrative.[12]

The narrative position of the church within the biblical narrative elicits typological readings as the church seeks to witness to Christ as the people of God in anticipation of the end of creation, its telos. Therefore, "figural interpretation is nothing less or more than a means of carrying forward the biblical story into the present and the future."[13]

The biblical narrative replaces the story of individual salvation and

---

[9]Milbank, "Name of Jesus," p. 150.

[10]Charles L. Campbell, *Preaching Jesus: New Directions for Homiletics in Hans Frei's Postliberal Theology* (Grand Rapids: Eerdmans, 1997), p. 253.

[11]For an argument that the spiritual meaning is necessary to sustain the unity of the Scriptures by finding its unity in Jesus Christ, see Henri De Lubac, "The Unity of the Two Testaments," in *Medieval Exegesis: The Four Senses of Scripture* (Grand Rapids: Eerdmans, 1998), 1:225-67.

[12]Campbell, *Preaching Jesus*, p. 251.

[13]Ibid.

the story of the state in relationship to the church. The centrality of the church in the biblical narrative moves us out of the story of the individual seeking his or her own individual salvation and the story of the moral reformation of the nation as the elect people of God. The individual finds salvation through Christ as a member of Christ's body, the church, the elect people of God. Even while the nation parodies the life of the church in its claim for the allegiance of its citizens, the church becomes a witness to the nation to show the nature of God's genuine intent for all creation through the life of its citizens (Phil 3:20).[14] Even though God has revealed the end of the narrative in the coming of Christ, the narrative still unfolds before us in our world, our lives and our congregations.

Embracing a tragic moment so that North American Christians might hear the good news anew means embracing the church as the place from which we interpret the Scriptures. Only preaching from within the church can form a people into the faithful character that the Holy Spirit seeks to call forth through the Scriptures. Because of the place of the church within the biblical narrative, we can retrieve the biblical narrative only as we retrieve the theological role of the church as a particular people as well.

The biblical narrative is very concrete and communal—it informs us about specific characters that God calls forth to form a faithful, obedient people among the nations. God sent forth the Son to die on a cross in order to redeem and form such a people. This shows the utter seriousness that God has for the role of the church within creation. Since this cuts against the grain of the predominant narratives that support North American culture, the preacher must develop special rhetorical tactics to move the congregation again and again back into the biblical narrative. The preacher must learn to move and to turn in order to overcome these cultural overhangs, much as in rock climbing.

---

[14]For the nation as a parody of the church see William T. Cavanaugh, "The City: Beyond Secular Parodies," in *Radical Orthodoxy: A New Theology,* ed. John Milbank, Graham Ward and Catherine Pickstock (London: Routledge, 1999), pp. 182-200. For the political implications of Philippians 3:20, see Richard A. Horsley, "General Introduction," in *Paul and Empire: Religion and Power in Roman Imperial Society,* ed. Richard A. Horsley (Harrisburg, Penn.: Trinity Press International, 1997), pp. 1-8.

Preaching into an Epistemological Crisis: A Rhetoric of Turning

Inductive preaching has recently reinvigorated homiletics. As shown by
Charles Campbell, such a homiletic is deeply embedded in an "experi-
ential-expressivist" theology that never really moves beyond the contemporary experience of an individual.[15] Campbell writes, "in its focus on
the individual, 'private' experiential event, contemporary homiletics has
itself succumbed to the 'tyranny' of American culture over the individual,
which inhibits the hearing of the gospel."[16] In its search for relevance
most inductive preaching, in theory and practice, reinforces the cultural
status quo, even if it can occasionally adopt a countercultural language.
Inductive preaching can give the illusion of ascending to the top of a
precipice, yet it always returns to the same place at the base of the cliff,
merely changing the name of the base through the sermon.[17]

As Campbell recognizes, however, the narrative shift in preaching
has marked a substantial rhetorical improvement over older cognitive-
propositional models. Cognitive-propositional models give congregations moralizing instruction or propositions to assent to in a rational,
logical order. Because of the contemporary cultural emphasis on experience, the propositional nature of such preaching can sound—and often
is claimed—to be countercultural itself.[18] The problem, however, is that
the narrative convictions of a congregation remain unengaged in such
models. Information might accrue on top of convictions like layers of
varnish on an old piece of furniture. Such a rhetoric provides no means
to encounter the deepest convictions of a congregation. The preacher
builds on top of the convictions that the congregation already has. Christianity becomes a belief or moral system for cognitive assent.

---

[15]For Campbell's full analysis see his *Preaching Jesus,* pp. 117-86.

[16]Ibid., p. 144.

[17]See, i.e., David Buttrick, who combines a rhetoric method to support a theological anthropol-
ogy as a foundation for preaching. Jesus is not a unique, unsubstitutable, irreplaceable character in God's story of redemption for Buttrick but a "living symbol" that discloses "in himself
the presence of *Gratuitous Love*" (David Buttrick, *Homiletic: Moves and Structures* [Philadel-
phia: Fortress, 1987], p. 15).

[18]This is seen, for instance, the work of John F. MacArthur, *Ashamed of the Gospel: When the
Church Becomes Like the World* (Wheaton, Ill.: Crossway Books, 1993). I share a certain sympathy with MacArthur's concerns, but I believe that the emphasis on right belief over embodiment of the Scriptures represents as much of an accommodation to the modernist culture as
those whom he criticizes.

Cognitive-propositional preaching leads a congregation to agree with the Scriptures rather than embody them. Such preaching demands the assent of an intellect, not the formation of bodies and affections in a particular way within a particular community called the church. The life of the Christian becomes reduced to right belief. Even demons might agree with cognitive-prepositional preaching, but nonetheless, remain demons (Jas 2:19)! A deductive, cognitive-propositional rhetoric will not re-place a congregation into the biblical narrative as the pilgrim people of God.

Campbell's theological analysis correctly calls us to embrace a new, Christologically based preaching. Yet he never concretely suggests a rhetoric for moving a congregation into the biblical narrative. Much as Barth decried rhetoric in preaching (with a very powerful rhetoric, one might add!), Campbell leaves the reader with an abstract theological demand without a means of turning a congregation into the biblical text. This is the lacuna that I would like to fill. We must think tactically rather than strategically.[19] We will remove current inductive homiletic rhetoric from its experiential/anthropological theological commitments and use it to move congregations from the dominant narratives of the culture into the biblical narrative. We need to subvert the theological commitments of contemporary inductive homiletics by developing a homiletic of turning or repentance.

Much like we saw in rock climbing, there are at least two separate

---

[19]For the distinction between strategy and tactics, see Michel de Certeau, *The Practice of Everyday Life* (Berkeley: University of California Press, 1984). He writes, "I call a 'strategy' the calculus of force relationships which becomes possible when a subject of will and power (a proprietor, an enterprise, a city, a scientific institution) can be isolated from an 'environment.' A strategy assumes a place that can be circumscribed as *proper (propre)* and thus serve as the basis for generating relations with an exterior distinct from it (competitors, adversaries, 'clienteles,' 'targets,' or 'objects' of research). Political, economic, and scientific rationality has been constructed on this strategic model.

"I call a 'tactic,' on the other hand, a calculus which cannot count on a 'proper' (a spatial or institutional localization), nor thus on a borderline distinguishing the other as a visible totality. The place of a tactic belongs to the other. A tactic insinuates itself into the other's place, fragmentarily, without taking it over in its entirety, without being able to keep it at a distance. It has at its disposal no base where it can capitalize on its advantages, prepare its expansions, and secure independence with respect to circumstances. The 'proper' is a victory of space over time. On the contrary, because it does not have a place, a tactic depends on time—it is always on the watch for opportunities that must be seized 'on the wing.' Whatever it wins, it does not keep. It must constantly manipulate events in order to turn them into 'opportunities.' The weak must continually turn to their own ends forces alien to them" (ibid., p. xix).

concepts inherent within the notion of turning. To turn requires that something moves—people cannot turn unless they are moving. Static proclamations cannot transfer congregations from one underlying narrative into a different narrative. Preaching a homiletic of repentance requires that a sermon move as well.

While turning is a type of motion, it is also motion of a particular kind. Turning in rock climbing requires movement in at least three different directions. On the face of a rock, a turn presupposes that the climber is first headed in a particular direction. When faced with an obstacle overhead, he or she acknowledges it and drives an anchor. The climber is now free to pivot and move horizontally safely. When the horizontal move is complete, the climber can again drive a new anchor and turn again, ascending to new vistas. Similarly, a homiletic of turning involves (1) acknowledgement of the contemporary horizon of a congregation as they have been formed by the culture, (2) an anchor to move horizontally around the contemporary horizon, and (3) heading in the new direction toward the summit. The sermon must move into the point of turning, the tragic moment, but it cannot stay there. The sermon must point beyond the tragic loss of previous narratives by traversing them, pointing the congregation into the wonderful good news of living amid God's story.

A Moving Rhetoric: Moves Versus Points

In the contemporary world, consensus in any area of theological discourse remains elusive. Yet major homiletical thought and instruction in recent decades have reached a consensus about at least one thing. Eugene Lowry informs us that recent major homileticians "all refuse to announce a conclusion in advance, all 'keep the cat in the bag,' all are mobile, moving sequenced forms, which involve a strategic delay of the preacher's meaning. In quite different ways, and yet related, they all involve some kind of 'plot.'"[20] Sermons now are narratives that require movement along a plot line.

If a preacher shifts the narrative horizons in which human beings live,

---

[20]Eugene Lowry, *The Homiletical Plot: The Sermon as Narrative Art Form* (Atlanta: John Knox Press, 1980), p. 28.

the concept of homiletical movement is a necessity, not a luxury. Structuring sermons that move must not serve as a mere rhetorical ploy to induce an "aha" moment for the congregation. Movement is essential to work within, out of and into different narratives in order to shift the narrative horizons of a congregation.

To shift convictions, preachers structure sermons to denaturalize the narratives that a congregation has learned from the culture. At that point the congregation might experience the difference that is necessary to live within the biblical narrative, God's story. By constructing sermons that move, the congregation may at least hear the possibility of a new place, a new culture called the church that restructures all of life. By embracing moves, a sermon might move up to the cultural obstacle, explicate it, traverse it and then point the way upward. Sermons that move possess the potentiality to engage a congregation at the levels of their deepest commitments and allegiances, in other words, at the level of their faith.

In order to grasp the significance of moves, it is helpful to step back and take a look what actually takes place in all sermons. David Buttrick correctly claims that "sermons, no matter how intricately arranged, involve sequential talking, a series of language modules put together by some sort of logic."[21] Understanding that any sermon involves a sequential pattern of speaking can help us differentiate between a sermon structured by the logic of *moves* from a sermon constructed on the logic of *points*.

The sequential logic of moves differs from that of points much like climbing a rock differs from climbing the rungs of a ladder. A move requires attention to the transition from one place to another. When a family moves, they gather all their belongings into one place, mindful of their destination, so that when they arrive at their new home, life might resume as quickly as possible into a normal routine. Moves have a goal or an end that we must always bear in mind, even as we gather in one place before moving on. Moves require an employment, a narrative development, a journey. The logic of moves begins at one place, but even as we gather, it requires that we look ahead to the destination we are moving to.

---

[21]Buttrick, *Homiletic*, p. 24.

The sequential logic of points differs. Points provide stability; they presuppose solid ground that all might stand on and return to. When someone climbs a ladder, he or she secures the base from which to scramble directly upward. If the base is stable and the rungs good, the journey is quickly completed in order to survey the situation from the top of the ladder. Similarly, when a driver pulls to the side of the road to look over a scenic point, he or she stands and gazes, but does not explore or embark on a journey. The person can look in different directions to view the full panorama. Yet he or she does so only to construct a single picture, not to tell a story.

A point is static and immobile. We climb ladders and then descend to the very place that we began. The work done on top is the crucial point, surveying the scene from multiple angles to analyze a single problem. A pastor preaches in points to develop a thesis, to describe a setting. Each point fills out a different aspect of the same fundamental view. A series of points produce an image like a portrait, an image within an already given, single frame of reference. Points presuppose the stability of the base, an unshakeable foundation from which to ascend the rungs of the ladder to glimpse the view from the top before returning to the *terra firma*, which is shared by all.

The concept of moves provides an opportunity for a homiletic of turning that points do not have. Within a sequential logic of moves, a preacher can generate difference at the deepest levels of a congregation's convictions. Within a sequential logic of points, a preacher can only *declare* difference. Moves can take a congregation on an expedition so that the deepest differences of place might be *explored, felt* and *experienced.* Points can only describe different places from the outside for an observer to accept or reject. Moves allow a sermon to develop as a guided tour to different places that might be experienced. Points structure a sermon like slides taken from a single location and then projected on a common screen.

Moves help us explore a terrain from within before journeying to a new place to explore difference. The mobility provided by structuring a sermon according to moves helps connect a sermon with congregational expectations. To connect with a congregation, however, does not mean that we merely rearticulate what the congregation has already experienced, now baptized with certain theological significance. In structuring a sermon by moves, we can begin with an inductive moment within the congregation's expectations. We can embrace a common culturally formed experience as a meeting place with the congregation. This is the strength of inductive preaching, of preaching from and to the experience of the congregation as it has been formed by the North American culture.

However, other places exist outside the congregation's given experience. This is why embracing moves rather than points can help a preacher to renarrate human lives in a manner that points cannot. Moves allow a preacher to establish a common narrative horizon with the congregation. A preacher can explore this place, image it, articulate its presuppositions and implications, resonate with the experiences that such narratives have formed within the congregation.

With moves, however, we do not have to end where we began. We do not have to stay at the meeting place with a congregation. We can begin with a congregation at a commonly constructed place without remaining at that place. We do not have to bow to current congregational horizons as an idol that the gospel must serve. Moves permit us to find a place to begin, but more, it allows reflection on the final narrative end of the sermon—the place where the narrative hopes to transport the congregation.

Homiletical mobility afforded by the concept of moves becomes increasingly important as the North American society continues to drift into a post-Christian era. We rarely encounter the problem that the biblical narrative is too familiar and thus needs to be reawakened from its latency through rhetorical surprise. Our problem is that people no longer have access to the fundamental language and grammar of the Christian faith. Biblical language is strange, unknown territory, often even for those who have lived long within the church.

The homiletic strategy of translating the Scriptures into the congregational life through a comedic moment has compounded the problem. Such an apologetic approach ultimately requires the preacher to shift narratives out of the biblical narrative and language, and thus to radically change the meaning of biblical language. The Scriptures become co-opted by other narratives and other polities than the church. Merely speaking in points from on high is not helpful either. Without some means of connecting with the congregation, words can vanish mid-air before reaching the congregation. A congregation might acknowledge the point, even agree with it, but not experience it as fundamentally different from the convictions that shape their lives.

Preexisting differences between the biblical and other narratives must be not only stated but experienced. Recent research into learning has highlighted the importance of addressing preconceptions that people bring into a learning situation:

> Drawing out and working with existing understandings is important for learners of all ages. Numerous research experiments demonstrate the persistence of preexisting understandings among older students even after a new model has been taught that contradicts the naïve understanding.[22]

Human beings live habitually. Cultural convictions are deeply embedded in the bodies of a gathered congregation—everything in the culture around them works to make such convictions seem "natural." To allow the congregation to be formed as a peculiar people, to allow the biblical narrative "to replace the naïve understanding, students [congregants] must reveal the latter [their previous understanding] and have the opportunity to see where it falls short."[23] We must embrace this tragic moment of difference if repentance is to occur.

Our post-Christian environment provides a challenge and opportunity for the preacher. This setting allows the preacher to present the genuine difference between the biblical narrative and the narratives of the culture for a congregation to hear. Rather than coasting on the narrative presuppositions of the reigning culture, the preacher may engage the congregation and then turn them to form the church as a peculiar people, living within the biblical narrative as a sign of God's redemptive intent for all creation.

A First Step: Expressing the "Natural"—the Status Quo Move

A homiletic of turning requires a commitment to the concept of moves. Movement, however, is not sufficient in and of itself to place a congre-

---

[22]John D. Bransford et al., eds., *How People Learn: Brain, Mind, Experience and School* (Washington, D.C.: National Academy Press, 2000), pp. 15-16.
[23]Ibid., p. 16.

gation into the biblical narrative. Movement can lead to a variety of places for different purposes. For instance, a soccer player will attempt various moves according to their situation on the field. With no one between the player and the goalie, the player will move straight toward the goal to attempt to score. At midfield, however, a player may reverse the ball with a long pass to the other side of the field in order to go around rather than go through the defense. Likewise, preachers might construct moves to direct their congregation to the appropriate goal in a variety of ways.

Most narrative preaching bears the inductive commitments of moving from the specific to the general; it presupposes a linear logical sequence. Preachers plot complications or reversals, but plot them within the same narrative. The complications or reversals are designed to bring about surprise, the resolution of the plot in order to intensify the experience of the congregation. Experience is enriched, but fundamental narratives are not replaced. Like *I Love Lucy,* the plot's design is to resolve the story—a comedy.

Yet moves can change directions in more radical ways. Perhaps the appropriate move in response to the complications of an *I Love Lucy* episode is not to see how Lucy escapes the consequences of her bad judgment. Perhaps the right move is to change channels, or better, turn the television off to spend the evening working on homework with the children. While all plots involve movement and thus turning, turnings need not be merely within narratives. Movement can involve re-placement from one narrative to another. The difference between the biblical narrative and the narratives that guide the North American culture calls for a more radical turning between the plots that form human lives in today's world.

Even though turning off the television may be the appropriate response to the latest reality TV programming, we cannot walk into another person's living room, turn the TV off and say, Go work on homework together! Such an activity would justly produce hostility from parent and children alike, and removal from the house without an invitation to return. We live in a culture that prefers fun over work; it seems self-evident that *I Love Lucy* is fun and homework is, well, work. Deep interests have formed us to experience life in this way. Challenging this formation requires that we identify with its power yet be able to show why such a presupposition is not natural but is formed by interests that seek to undermine the long-term viability of life for those who live by them.

If we want to move a congregation into a different narrative world, we must first engage the interpretive horizons of the congregation as they have been formed by the society around them. We cannot, so to speak, homiletically walk into the living room and begin talking as if the television is not on, nor can we abruptly change the channel without explanation. The first move must establish common ground with the congregation; this should be familiar turf for all in the congregation. We enter the status quo not to embrace it but ultimately to reveal its difference from what will follow.

Beginning the sermon by moving into the "natural"—the status quo—produces at least two positive results. First, it allows the preacher to identify with the congregation and vice versa. The status quo provides a region of comfort in which preacher and congregation meet together on even footing. None of us have escaped formation of the narratives provided by North American culture. We've all laughed at *I Love Lucy* episodes. Banal though they may be, the power of TV programming is such that we find it difficult to turn it off or change channels in the middle of the program. Moving into the status quo provides a rhetorical connection between the congregation and the preacher.

Second, moving into the status quo sets the stage for the congregation to experience the difference that the biblical narrative makes. Surveying the cultural environment allows one to discover what appears "natural" for the congregation. Articulating what is presupposed will help remove obstacles so that the biblical text may speak Christianly. It will help the congregation differentiate cultural commitments whose origins lie in narratives that stand outside the biblical narrative. These commitments prohibit hearing the biblical text as a call to the unique formation of the church. By carefully developing this initial move, we can develop the horizons that provide the conditions for hearing the tragic moment as a genuine tragedy that has obscured the biblical text from being heard and embodied within the world.

Interpretive charity demands that we articulate these convictions in the strongest, most sympathetic terms possible.[24] It is important not to caricature, demean or misrepresent the societal convictions that have formed the congregation. In a very real sense, when preachers speak outside the biblical narrative, they speak as a guest in someone else's home. Even if it is the home of an enemy, Christians are called to nonetheless love their enemies. While preachers must recognize that they are called by the gospel to move the congregation in a different direction, they cannot celebrate the narrative malformation of congregation, especially as they recognize that this malformation cuts through their own bodies as well.

Beginning the sermon with a move into the status quo presupposes that we structure the sermon in a way other than linear development. A move into the "natural" sets up a sermon for a turn by providing a basis *from which* to turn. A sharp angle disturbs the linear development of the sermon. We can bring up an opposing conviction first so that the sermon—and the congregation—might be moved beyond it. Beginning the sermon with convictions formed outside the biblical narrative—the "natural"—helps to devise a homiletic tactic that engages the congregation where they are yet provides the capability to re-place them later into the biblical narrative.

This initial move demands that we can distinguish between the narrative formation *and* virtues of the society at large and those that emerge from the biblical narrative. A Christian form of cultural criticism needs to be practiced so that we, in an initial move, can avoid simplistic moralisms and instead address the fundamental convictions that shape lives formed by North American culture.

Obviously, I believe that narratives of individualism and the righteous nation are two fundamental narratives that consistently need to be contested if congregations are going to be formed into a peculiar people. Rather than working within the status quo to make a congregation part of a "kinder, gentler nation," we engage it so that the congregation might encounter its tragic nature, its difference, in relationship to the biblical text. Out of the differences between the narratives of the world and the

---

[24]For a discussion of interpretive charity, see Stephen E. Fowl, "Vigilant Communities and Virtuous Readers," in *Engaging Scripture* (Oxford: Blackwell, 1998), pp. 62-96, esp. pp. 91-95.

biblical narrative, the Spirit of God may thereby call forth a people shaped by the life, teachings, death and resurrection of Jesus Christ.

To form such an initial move, the preacher should state clearly and descriptively what appears to be natural to the congregation. Often such moves can begin with phrases like "We've been taught that . . ." or "We live in a world that thinks . . ." or "The society around us has formed us to believe that . . ." The congregation should hear the initial move as descriptive, not normative. If the congregation hears it as normative, they will become confused as the sermon moves in a different direction.

We should never sucker punch the congregation. While the initial move might evoke assent, such assent does not need to be encouraged by positive imagery. We need to present the status quo as descriptive of the narrative horizons of the society in which the church exists as strangers and aliens. The tone of the initial move should be neutral. The congregation will thus find themselves within the move, but their commitment to the status quo should not be reinforced.

As we develop a move into the status quo, we can even highlight contradictions or difficulties that such commitments bring with them. Underlying tensions can prepare a congregation to hear alternatives provided by the biblical narrative as the Spirit calls them to be distinctly formed as part of the people of God. The tragic moment is foreshadowed in these tensions, even as we charitably explicate the cultural commitments.

Finally, the initial move needs firm closure. As the rock climber must set an anchor before ascending again, preachers can easily close off the initial move by rephrasing the assertions that began the move. If a turning is to take place, the sermon must completely seal off the move. Then the congregation might hear and embrace the alternative found in the biblical narrative. The move must come to a complete stop, a clear termination so that the congregation will not anticipate continuing in the same direction.[25] Simple, descriptive language should characterize this conclusion. This move has explored the way that world depicts things—not how they actually are.

The following illustrates a move into the status quo. It is the first move

---

[25]David Buttrick writes, "The matter of closure is more important than we know. Moves start strongly and end with equal strength; they must 'round out' and conclude" (Buttrick, *Hermeneutic*, p. 52.)

of a sermon that images misconceptions about Christian holiness that arises from one of the deepest narratives that guide American culture— the narrative of the autonomous individual.

We have learned to place holiness in the choices we make as isolated, independent individuals. We've learned to grit our teeth, pull up our pants and step out as a solitary individual, my will in mortal combat against inward sin. It seems natural—if my individual choices are what really matter, holiness must reside in my choices.

Many of us, though not all, were born in the United States. We have had individualism deeply woven into us. Even more deeply, we think that being individual is opposed to being part of a community. The individual and community exist as two opposing poles. The more we are shaped by a community, the less we're supposedly individual; the more we are individuals, the less claims any community supposedly has on us. If we're going to make a trip, we think that we either have to do it alone or it won't be our trip.

We think this even though something within us knows it's just not true. Have you ever seen the movie *Cast Away?* Tom Hanks plays the part of a lone survivor on a deserted island. Loneliness eats him up. He desperately needs companionship. Alone on an island, his whole sense of self is eaten away. He finds a volleyball and draws a face on it with his own blood. He calls it "Wilson." Wilson becomes the castaway's community. The message is clear: To survive, humans need other human beings. To be human is to be surrounded by other humans. Therefore, it is stunning how the movie ends. Remember? The castaway is rescued, returns to society and tries to rebuild his life. In the closing scene, the former castaway stands alone, isolated, all by himself as an individual, at a crossroads in the middle of nowhere. His future depends on his choice. Will he remain an isolated, independent individual? He makes his choice; the movie ends. The scene violates everything the movie has shown. The man is not an isolated individual. His life is not about his independent choices. His life only makes sense within a community of others, even if it was only Wilson.

Friends, if we are going to make the trek toward holiness, if God's grace is going to work in us, cleansing, rewiring, reforming us, we are going to have to reject a crass individualism that sees holiness merely in our choices, in what happens to us as individuals, in our own trip, a trek we make as independent, rational, isolated individuals. It is not individual versus community. No! We have to reject the opposition. Community allows us to be individuals; the church gives us choices that we wouldn't otherwise have. Yes, we make choices as individuals; yes, of course we do. But no, you never make the trek that is the Christian life as an isolated, rational, independent human being.

This is difficult to hear. We've been formed to think that we make the trek toward holiness as autonomous, independent human beings.

The move ties a misconception about Christian holiness, that holiness is largely a matter of the will, our choices as autonomous individuals, with concepts of the individual taken from American culture. The widely viewed movie *Cast Away* illustrates the point that communities create and sustain individuals, even as it showed the incoherence in American culture's convictions about how to be an individual. This initial move establishes a common place, that which is natural within the experience of the congregation, but it also unsettles this place, preparing the congregation for the turn that will follow. The congregation is prepared to recognize that they are called to live the Christian life not as Americans but as part of God's people called the church.

The opening move into the status quo is a significant way to highlight the position the congregation must move from. Articulating the narrative status quo prepares the congregation for the tragic moment, the tragedy that our lives are formed by stories other than God's, a formation that makes it difficult if not impossible to hear the Scriptures as Christians. Nevertheless, discovering that the tragic has shaped us is good news for Christians, for God offers humans a better way as participants in God's story. Status quo narratives name what must be left behind as God calls the church to live its unique, elect witness in the world. Yet the mere naming of the cultural status quo will not create a turn in and of itself. The tragic also needs to be named.

The Tragic and the Announcement of Good News:
The Transition Paragraph

Marching bands make sharp, precise turns. A band member steps forward with the right foot, pivots on the ball of the foot and heads in a new direction, stepping out with the left. Attempting such a sharp turn homiletically, however, will leave the congregation marching straight ahead while the preacher swings in a different direction, like a drum major who mistakenly turns away from the band. Soon it becomes apparent to all that the drum major and the band are performing two different routines. Confusion, not difference, emerges. A homiletic of turning requires careful transition into and out of the tragic moment so that the congregation might hear the call into the biblical narrative.

It is possible to turn a sermon so that the preacher and the congregation stay in step with each other. The key is to construct an appropriate transition.[26] To turn a congregation within a sermon requires a separate paragraph. We need to be careful not to expand the transition into a whole move. Yet the transition requires particular attention. The transitional paragraph must fulfill three separate functions. It needs to (a) close the previous move, (b) declare the bankruptcy of the status quo, and (c) announce another way, the way of good news.

In closing the previous move, we must simply and briefly reiterate the previous move with one or, at most, two sentences. We should not develop the previous move any more, but merely point the congregation's attention to what has already been said. After the natural pause following the closure of the previous move, the congregation will expect the sermon to progress. The reiteration of the previous move will cause them to reflect on what has just been said.

Now comes the crucial turn of the sermon—the moment of the tragic. After working within the interpretive horizons provided by the culture, we must declare clearly—but compassionately—the incompatibility of the previous move with the life of the church formed by the biblical narrative. We must kindly but firmly bring the direction of the previous move to a halt. To turn, the anchor must be driven and the guide must point to foot- and handholds above.

Being told you're wrong is never fun; the preacher should not exalt in the moment. Gloating within the tragic moment is entirely inappropriate. It is extremely important that the preacher identify with the congregation in their (mal)formation by the culture. "Speaking the truth in love" demands that as we turn the congregation, naming the idols of their—and our own—lives, we do so in a manner that empowers the congregation to move into the biblical narrative with us. The goal is positive; the preacher does not seek to evoke resentment against the past

---

[26]Buttrick discusses a similar homiletical situation when he speaks of connecting separate sets of moves. He writes, "When sets join, the connection will require much more focus than the joining of sequential moves. Thus, the closure of a final move in a set will probably require several sentences, and the opening of a following move will have to be equally emphatic—perhaps using five sentences to establish the move statement. . . . Where two different sets bump together, extra strength will have to be built into the connective logic that joins the sets together" (ibid., p. 77). Buttrick correctly notes that the larger the homiletical transition, the more careful attention and time needs devoted to take the congregation through the transition.

horizons of the congregant's lives. The congregation must perceive the turning to be for their benefit, not as retaliation drawn from pastoral defensiveness or ire. The preacher must help the congregation recognize that convictions drawn from outside the biblical narrative will not empower their sanctification or witness.

Turning demands more than renouncing the past direction. An authentic transition does not merely look backward and deny the legitimacy of the past; it must also stake out the path ahead, declaring the good news of a different way. We believe that the gospel is true; it is natural. It only seems countercultural because of the formative powers of the culture around us.

Immediately following the declaration of the nonviability of the false conviction for the Christian, the preacher announces a better way, good news, a direction of hope for the congregation. He or she announces that we need not live in the convictions provided by the society at large so that we can live truthfully within God's story. The preacher may then proceed with an introductory statement of the next move. This will finish the turn and prepare the congregation to go with the preacher as they move together into the biblical narrative.

In the previous sermon illustration on 2 Timothy, I developed a move that declared that a person cannot experience the sanctifying grace of God as an isolated, autonomous individual. A transition summary is needed now to provide the turn and direct the congregation into a place, their own congregational life, where they can hear the biblical text as Christians:

Transition summary:

> We simply can't make the trip toward holiness as rugged, American individualists. We can't let the story that our society has told us—that the world has ground into us—draw this massive line between being an individual and being part of a community. We can't. We can't because it's just not true. Deep down we know it's not true. And unless we recognize its falsity, we won't be able to hear the Scriptures this morning. The Scriptures point us to another way, a way that is good news, a way that takes us into the fullness of life that is lived as part of the people of God. We can't make the trip alone, and the good news is that we don't have to! God calls us into the fullness of the life of faith among the faithful.

The transition summarizes the previous move that explored the status quo. It declares that such a conviction provides an obstacle to the faithful Christian life, and it turns the congregation in a different direction, a direction within the life of the church as the people of God.

A homiletic of turning requires a pivot, the redirection of a congregation by shifting its narrative horizons from that provided by the society to the narrative horizon of the Scriptures, embodied within the church. A simple transition paragraph can summarize the previous move, declare its problematic status, and point in a new direction. Such a transition paragraph frees a congregation to hear the difference that God has made through the gift of the Son. The congregation can then hear the Spirit's call to live as part of a specific, concrete people of God, shaped by the biblical story.

Moving into God's Story

Once we have turned, only one task remains—to set out in a new direction! Having traversed obstacles so that the Scriptures might be heard, we now can proclaim the good news, calling people into God's story as part of the people of God living from the life, death and resurrection of Christ into the consummation of the ages in Christ's return. Old things are left behind as we head into the new!

The preacher is now free to speak from within the presuppositions that render the Bible coherent as the Christian Scriptures: the life of the church. We may use all the rhetorical skills possible to construct the move to lead the people into the text. The goal is not to elicit what is already present, though unformed, in the congregation's consciousness but rather to open a new possibility for life. By fleshing out with concrete imagery the life that the biblical narrative calls forth, the Spirit can re-form a congregation to embody the Scriptures.

As we work within God's story as the place for hearing the biblical text, we draw a clear distinction with what has gone before but does not go back. We do not set ourself to the plow and then turn back. Let bygones be bygones! The goal always stands ahead in the future life of the congregation, not in its past life shaped by the presuppositions of contemporary society. At present, this future might only exist in the our imagination and prayers. We must therefore always image life within the biblical narrative with a vividness and concreteness that exceeds the move into the status quo.

The pastor seeks to open a space within the congregation's imagination that can then become occupied in the future. He or she can do this by re-placing individual and congregational into the biblical narrative. In the process the biblical narrative reinterprets the significance of concrete everyday life. At this point telling stories from the lives of the saints—local, contemporary and historical—comes in handy. Stories of the saints show that the biblical narrative can be lived in its concrete reality as a visible witness. It is extremely important that the Christian life not be left as an abstraction; it is life within a concrete people, witnessing to God's intent for all creation as we await God's kingdom to come on earth as it is in heaven.

After moving through the status quo and a transitional summary, the sermon from 2 Timothy may now move the congregation into a place where they can hear the biblical text as defining their Christian life in the past so that they might live into God's future.

We make the trek toward holiness in the company of the faithful. The Christian life is not just about our own personal faith but the faith given to us by God through the saints, those who go before and with us. The faith we receive is the same faith that is lived by those who have already traveled with us as part of the people of God.

Early in *Lord, Teach Us* by Stanley Hauerwas and Will Willimon, the authors write: "Think of Christianity, not primarily as a set of doctrines, a volunteer organization, or a list of appropriate behaviors. Think of Christianity as naming a journey of a people."[27] Even more, think of Christianity as a pilgrim people that God called you to join, one person among a people that was pursuing the way before you even came along. As part of this people, you now make the journey.

You don't start the trip yourself. The Christian life is not just my trip or your trip. The Christian life didn't begin when I started. I was called into something already in progress. God had already called God's people into existence in the promise to Abraham. God had already called Israel to be a holy people, a kingdom of priests at Sinai. But that's not all. God had already opened this people to Gentiles in the life, death and resurrection of Jesus. The trek to holiness has been in progress in the life of the church across the ages. God has kept God's people moving toward the goal. Sometimes the church has been more faithful than at other times; sometimes it has horribly failed in its witness, but God's Spirit continuously calls new generations into the journey. Now here we are.

---

[27]William H. Willimon and Stanley Hauerwas, *Lord, Teach Us: The Lord's Prayer and the Christian Life* (Nashville: Abingdon, 1996), p. 13.

We are here because God has called us into the journey, into the adventure. God has called us as individuals to the journey through others. Think of those whose witness affected you to join the march, or whose witness right now is calling you. But that's not all. God surrounds us with the company of others, pilgrims making the same trip with us. And, miracle of miracles, God surrounds others with us, with me, sinful but forgiven and cleansed, on a journey, moving on and on. We individuals make the trek toward holiness as part of the broader march, the longer march for the fullness of God's kingdom, as part of the people of God, the church.

Don't believe me? Look at 2 Timothy 1:5. Here Paul speaks of the sincere faith of Timothy—he's on his way; he's in the journey. It is Timothy's faith; Timothy, a named, particular individual. But it's not merely Timothy's faith. The faith is also Lois's faith, his mother's faith. Timothy's faith is Lois's; her witness has transferred faith to him. But whose faith is Lois's? It's not merely her own. It's Eunice's, Timothy's grandmother. Whose faith is it? Timothy's? Yes! Lois's? Yes! Eunice's? Yes. And Eunice's faith was someone's before her, and then before her, until, finally, we find the origins of this faith. We find the origin of our faith in Jesus: Jesus' faithfulness on the cross. Timothy's faith, our faith, is ultimately found in the faithfulness of Jesus.

The trip, our trip, my very personal trip, is a trip that takes place, and only takes place, in the context of the people of God, the church.

This move takes the congregation into the biblical text by imaging the gift of faith, received by members within the congregation, as finding its origins in the faith of others, as Timothy's faith had its origin in those who came before him. Individual faith is not opposed to the community but comes to fruition through the faith-full lives of the saints. The individuals within the congregation become characters in the ongoing narrative of God's story of God's people.

A homiletic of turning ultimately needs to move a congregation out of narratives provided by the society at large and into the biblical narrative through the life, death and resurrection of Jesus Christ. The fusion of horizons does not come through collapsing the biblical text into the life of the individual or the nation. The sermon places the individual as a character within the unfolding narrative of God's story. The turn is now complete. The sermon frees the congregation to live as a peculiar people, who are witnesses to God's kingdom that has drawn near to us in Jesus Christ.

Resisting Temptation: Avoiding Rhetorical Pratfalls

How a congregation will receive a homiletic of turning will depend on the depth and "Christianness" of its moral commitments. How a pastor can help the congregation to be formed to receive such preaching will be discussed in chapter five. Yet I need to take a few moments to highlight rhetorical pratfalls that can doom a homiletic of turning even as it is practiced.

First, sermon structures must embrace clarity, especially between moves and within transitions. Clear introductory statements and clear statements of closure allow the congregation to move with the preacher. The same is true of our transitions. We need not offend people, but we must clearly state the difference to allow the congregation to follow the turn. To experience the tragic moment, difference must be embraced. This is frightening both for the preacher and the congregation, but genuine turning requires it. Clarity in repentance is necessary. The turn is not the place to be "nice"; too much is at stake.

Second, preachers must avoid trying to move too fast and do too much in the sermon. It takes time for the congregation to explore the narratives of the society and to absorb the turn to the biblical narrative. Time pressures often force preachers to move too fast; theological pressures sometimes force pastors to try to do too much. Our homiletical strategy needs to take into account how far the congregation can move, following the turn, in order to absorb its full implications. We cannot establish any hard and fast rule; it depends on the congregation's moral and theological formation. Congregations living within the biblical narrative can move more quickly through the turn—often brief status-quo moments are enough to remind them of the difference that they already experience. Congregations who are more closely aligned with society will need more time to go through the turn. The difference generated by the turn itself will need to sink in. To move too quickly will merely obscure the turn that has been made.

Finally, preachers must avoid turning a congregation Sunday after Sunday. Like a vaccine, a continual homiletic of turning will inoculate the congregation to difference rather than enabling them to comprehend it. Certain seasons of the church year are appropriate for such a homiletic—the Advent and Lenten seasons, seasons of repentance come most clearly to mind. Given the barrage of the society's narratives, the congregation needs to be reminded of the difference of their convictions. There is no substitute for pastoral discernment and wisdom in encouraging a congregation to embrace the difference of living within the biblical narrative.

Conclusion

The signs are all around us. We are living in a post-Christian situation in North America. Society at large lives by different interpretive narrative horizons than the church, narrative horizons that are as powerful as they are pervasive. Churches that accommodate these cultural horizons hang tenuously to the faith. The demise of American Christendom allows us to recognize that such enculturization has damaged the ongoing witness of the church as a visible body of Christ in the world. The church's visible witness lies in its ability to be distinctively Christian, different from the world for the sake of the world, different because we live out of a different story, God's story, as embedded in the Scriptures.

Pastors can establish connections with their congregation by moving within deep cultural convictions of the world. The move into the status quo brings to the surface an opposition that prevents a congregation from living within the biblical narrative. Next, a summary transition declares false the conviction formed by the society at large. Then we can pivot the congregation to a better way, the way of discipleship by living within the biblical narrative. Now the pastor is free to call the congregation to be formed by the biblical narrative in its concrete particularity and thus to embody the text in individual and communal witness as the distinct people of God in the world.

A homiletic of turning is nothing more than the homiletical structure practiced by Jesus in the Sermon on the Mount: "You have heard it said, . . . but I say to you . . ." This is how the church should live, not hiding its light under a basket but allowing its distinctiveness to shine in the world. Like salt and yeast, it might not look very impressive to those formed by the convictions of this age, but the concrete, embodied life of this particular people will pervade a world that desperately needs to see another way of living.

4

WEAVING THE STORY

Sermonic Exhibits

Preaching is always embedded in a concrete, particular historical situation. A sermon is never an end in itself, but finds its end in the formation of a congregation. Challenging contemporary cultural norms, not just those of the society at large but also within a congregation, demands pastoral discernment. Therefore, I present the following sermonic exhibits with some hesitancy. By "textualizing" these sermons, I displace them from their settings in the life of a particular congregation.

Nonetheless, I hope that the rhetorical strategy of chapter three will be clarified through these four sermons. Each sermon begins with a brief introduction; within the first three I provide comments on rhetorical tactics and theological content utilized. The common concern of these sermons is to realign a congregation within the biblical narrative so that the Spirit might form them into a distinct, peculiar people. The sermons engage a homiletic of turning to recast the narrative and communal framework of the congregation's life.

Sermon 1: What Really Matters (Gal 5:4-6)

North American Protestant Christianity has tended to develop a theology of works that either seeks to engage social structures to establish a more "just" society or to improve conditions for disadvantaged individuals through volunteer services. Works are separated from the working out of one's salvation, and placed in the public realm, a type of social witness in the world to which Christians are called. The following sermon tries to remove Paul's teaching about faith from an individualized covenant of grace and place it within a narrative setting where faith and works no longer oppose each other but come together as the ecclesial witness to the new creation. It begins by the entering the realm of "personal values," which transforms the whole society into consumers, and contrasts that with the Pauline vision of the new creation found within the body of Christ that maintains its witness by the faithfulness of Jesus— the faith that works by love. The sermon begins with a strong tragic move but also uses tragic moments in other moves to clarify the Pauline concept of faith from a common misinterpretation.

> What really matters? We live our life as an answer to that question. What does it mean to live a human life truthfully? How Christians conceive what matters makes all the difference in the world. How any human being lives life is always an answer to what really matters. In the book of Galatians, Paul thought he knew what matters. Let's take a look at how "what really matters" addresses us today.

The introduction does not try to do too much. It does what an introduction should do: it introduces. It briefly attempts to frame the issue as a basic issue that all humans must face. The next-to-last sentence informs the congregation that the Galatians text provides the basis for the sermon so that they are prepared when the sermon turns to the text from its initial explorations. The last sentence transitions the sermon toward the first move that will explore how a particular cultural narrative has formed us to think about the goals for our lives.

> What really matters? We've been taught by our society that the world is full of options. Take your pick; you can choose for yourself what really matters. Hey, it's a buyer's market. We've heard that what really matters is up to us—we can pick as we like. Our world has taught us that "one size does not fit all"—discover whatever brings you fulfillment and go for it—that's what really matters.
>
> We've all been taught that what really matters is itself a matter of values. We all know that values matter; we've been told that values are personal, individual, up to the freedom of each individual to find for him- or herself. What really matters is the ability of each individual to make up his or her mind about what really matters!
>
> Money—why not? Career. Status. Hey, it's up to you. Family. Relationships— if that sends you, fine. Jesus. If Jesus works for you, why not? You are allowed all the personal faith you need. A little spirituality is always helpful. What really

matters, we've been taught, is that we're free consumers—pick what you want, just as long as it doesn't infringe on anyone else's pursuit of what really matters to them.

And so we enter an endless search for fulfillment to serve our own inner needs—money, careers, relationships, hobbies, partying, Jesus, whatever. That's what we've been told life is about—our individual search for meaning, for value, for what matters. The problem is, what matters only matters to an individual. If what matters fits into no larger story than some individual desire, then what matters seems trivial, an empty category to pursue for one's own life.

What really matters, so our society has taught us, is anything that we decide matters, just as long as it doesn't get in the way of anyone else pursuing what really matters to them.

This first move tries to develop what I have described in chapter two, with Alasdair MacIntyre, as emotivism. It takes a lighthearted approach, a laissez-faire attitude that our society calls "toleration."[1]

Summary transition. Insofar as we've been shaped by our society, we've learned that what really matters is up to each one of us. Yet when we think about what really matters for a moment, we become uneasy. What really matters, it seems, must go beyond, transcend, merely fulfilling an individual. To really matter, something must be beyond mere personal preference. We recognize that something is wrong with this story; something is wrong even if we substitute good things into the underlying narrative. It is no surprise then that Paul has a different answer, an answer that points us in another direction.

While emotivism has deeply formed us, on reflection its intellectual problems become readily apparent. As D. Stephen Long writes, " 'Good' still seems to enchant us. . . . *Good* still signifies something more, something almost inexplicable, something enchanting."[2] The summary statement tries to raise homiletically the dis-ease that arises when "the good" is collapsed into personal subjectivity.

Paul is quite clear about what really matters: what really matters is faith working by love. The end, the purpose, of human life, according to Galatians, is faith

---

[1]See Jonathan Wilson, *Living Faithfully in a Fragmented World: Lessons for the Church from MacIntyre's After Virtue* (Harrisburg, Penn.: Trinity Press International, 1997), for a careful and creative interaction with MacIntyre for the life of the church.

[2]D. Stephen Long, *The Goodness of God: Theology, the Church, and Social Order* (Grand Rapids: Brazos, 2001), p. 31.

found active in love. It's not up to a vote or a consumer survey, friends: faith manifesting itself in love is what really matters for human lives.

Here we are in Galatians. Surely, Paul will tell us that what matters is faith alone! Only faith, assurance in Christ for my salvation, surely that is all that matters. An individual's own personal faith is what has to matter for Paul. But that's not what the text says. In Christ Jesus neither circumcision nor uncircumcision matters; the only thing that matters is faith working through love.

What's going on here? We have to remember that faith for Paul is not some inner conviction that God loves you. Faith is not merely some sort of cognitive assent. Faith is something much more specific, concrete, for Paul. Faith for Paul is trust and obedience, loyalty to God the Father, the One who raised Jesus Christ from the dead. *Faith* for Paul is a political term, a term that captures one's absolute allegiance to the God of Israel, the God of Jesus Christ. Since faith is a political word, there's no conflict between faith and works. Loyalties work or they aren't real loyalties. So faith works. But faith doesn't work in just any old way. Faith, loyalty to God, works by love, by giving oneself for the sake of others. Paul has no sense of sentimentality here. Faith, allegiance to Jesus is that which is actively shown in working for the sake of one's neighbor.

Recent Pauline scholarship has emphasized the political connotation of *pistis*. This becomes crucial to unpack the politics embedded in the passage. According to Dieter Georgi:

> "Faith" does not exhaust its meaning. "Faithfulness" or "loyalty," which includes the notion of "trust," comes nearer to the Pauline usage of the term. . . . Beginning in the time of Augustus, *fides,* the Latin synonym of *pistis,* was reassessed and assumed weightier dimensions.

The Caesar represented the *fides* of Rome in the sense of loyalty, faithfulness to treaty obligations, uprightness, truthfulness, honesty, confidence, and conviction—all, as it were, a Roman monopoly.[3]

By bringing out the social and political connotations of *pistis* as loyalty, the modernist split between faith as private and works as public disappears and the congregation may see that they have been led a false dichotomy between faith and works.

---

[3]Dieter Georgi, "God Turned Upside Down," in *Paul and Empire: Religion and Power in Roman Imperial Society,* ed. Richard A. Horsley (Harrisburg, Penn.: Trinity Press International, 1997), p. 149. Georgi is not idiosyncratic in this understanding; *pistis* seems related to a Old Persian word *bandaka.* "It is generally believe that the Classical vocabulary *(pistis/fides)* renders a Persian concept. . . . [A] *bandaka* was a person simultaneously subject and loyal to the king. The word *pistos* is probably not far removed" (Pierre Briant, *From Cyrus to Alexander: A History of the Persian Empire* [Winona Lake, Ind.: Eisenbrauns, 2002], pp. 324-25).

> Neither circumcision nor uncircumcision matters. What matters is faith, abso-
> lute trust, loyalty to God, energized by love, the giving of oneself for the sake
> of others. Where, friends, do we see most pure allegiance to God for the sake
> of others? Where do we see what really matters? We see it in the cross of Jesus
> Christ, who in obedience to God the Father, loved us and gave himself for us.
> What really matters, Paul is telling us, is the faith of Jesus Christ, the faith that
> brought forth our salvation, our participation in the people of God, a faith that
> we're called to share, to exhibit, a faith that obeys God, a faith manifested in
> love for others.
>
> What really matters, friends, is not just for me because I value it; but what
> really matters is faith working by love.

The rhetoric here reveals that contemporary emotivism cannot absorb
the Pauline text. This move is developed in contrast to the first move,
exploring the difference between living within the biblical narrative and
within the narratives provided by the contemporary culture.

> Why? Why does faith that works by love really matter? The faith that works by
> love matters because faith working by love shows forth the witness of the
> church as the bearers of God's new creation. Faith working by love shows the
> world what God will bring forth over all creation in the last day. The world can
> see in the concrete lives of a peculiar people what God desires—and will bring
> forth—from all creation, a people defined by faith working through love.
>
> Neither circumcision or uncircumcision counts for anything. Why would
> anyone think that circumcision or uncircumcision counts? Circumcision mat-
> ters if you are a Jew. It is Israel at stake here, those born of the seed of Abraham,
> those chosen by God to be a blessing to all nations. The issue here, for Paul, is
> the basis on which one becomes part of God's elect people; it's a sign that God
> is faithful to God's promises to Abraham. To what people do you belong? That's
> what really matters for Paul.
>
> Since God sent God's Son, Jesus Christ, neither circumcision nor uncircum-
> cision matters. In Jesus Christ, Gentiles now can take part in God's people. In
> Jesus' faithfulness, God has brought forth a new people as a witness to him, as
> a blessing to all nations. In Jesus' faith that works by love, we see the great in-
> vitation God has offered all humanity to join in God's elect people. What mat-
> ters now is not what mattered before the coming of Christ. What matters now
> is Jesus Christ, the faith that works by love that initiated a new age whereby we
> might live wholly for God, even amid the evil world around us. Faith working
> by love really matters because we are saved; we enter God's people through the
> faithfulness of Jesus!
>
> But that's not all. Faith working by love matters because such faith character-
> izes God's people, the body of Christ in the world. We too are called to partici-

pate in the faith of Jesus Christ, the faith that works by love. If our witness as God's people is going to be sustained, we must be so formed by the Spirit that our lives are lived in absolute allegiance to God shown in self-giving love for the sake of each other. That's how the church is sustained in its witness across time. The faith that works by love matters because God has gathered us together by God's grace so that individually and together as a community the world might see our lives and gain a glimpse of how God wants all creation to be. As Paul writes in Galatian 6:15, "Neither circumcision nor uncircumcision means anything; what really counts is new creation." The faith that works by love really matters because in the church's embodied witness to the faithfulness of Jesus, we participate in the new creation that God will bring forth in Christ's return.

What really matters, friends, is living the faithfulness of Jesus, the faith that works by love, in our lives with each other, amid a watching, waiting world.

This move tries to tie the believer's participation in the faith that works by love to its Christological basis within the biblical narrative. As Richard Hays writes, "The twin themes of conformity to Christ's death and the imitation of Christ are foundational elements of Paul's vision and moral life. . . . Obedience to God is defined paradigmatically . . . by Jesus' death on the cross."[4] Rather than a historical moment within the first century, the text sustains its call for members living within the same historical community still alive today.

Conclusion. What really matters? When do we find we are living our lives as God intended? In living as part of God's people, by faith working by love. Where can we find this faith? Look at the Table set before you. What do you see there? "This is my body, broken for you." "This is my blood, shed for you and for many for the forgiveness of sins." "Whenever you do this, do this in remembrance of me." Here, friends, we find God calling us to Jesus' faithfulness so that we might be made, in him, the body of Christ in the world. Here we may participate in the faith that works through love. Come, friends. Come and be thankful.

Sermon 2: An Agenda for a New Year (Eph 1:3-14)

The following sermon was preached on the happy convergence between the lectionary and the secular New Year. Of course, the Christian New Year begins on the first Sunday of Advent—Christ the King Sunday. Yet given the formative influence of the national calendar, the sermon

---

[4]Richard B. Hays, *The Moral Vision of the New Testament: Community, Cross, New Creation* (New York: HarperCollins, 1996), p. 31.

engaged the national "holiday" and then moved the congregation from a narrative embedded within the contemporary society to the narrative of the Scriptures. The sermon speaks from within a particular tradition, the Methodist-Holiness tradition initiated by the ministry and writings of John Wesley. The tradition-laden nature of the discourse, however, is not seen as a liability to distract from what the Scripture "really says" but as a means of opening the text to hear it anew.

Again the sermon is constructed with an initial tragic move, with tragic moments for reinforcement later on. It is rather aggressive, more so than the first sermon, in moving the congregation into the story of the individual, only to shift the categories into categories consistent with the biblical narrative. Yet its goal is the same: to move the congregation from the individual narrative of self-fulfillment, secular or "Christianized," into a biblical narrative where the believer stands as part of the people of God.

Introduction. This Scripture leaped out at me as powerful and beautiful for today. Now, I'm aware that you probably don't really care about theological traditions. But I am convinced there is truth to be found, insight into the gospel of Jesus Christ and its affect on our lives that we may discover, if we can hear a text amid the saints who've gone before us. Our Scripture reading from Ephesians this morning really comes alive when we read it from the perspective of an eighteenth-century English Christian named John Wesley. What I want to do is read this Scripture from Wesley's perspective to see if together we might set an agenda for our lives as we face the New Year.

1. With the turn of the New Year, we find an agenda in the greeting we give one another: Happy New Year! This little phrase states our dreams, our desire, the goal for our lives in the upcoming year. If there is one thing we want out of next year, we've been taught, it is a Happy New Year!

I'm fascinated how our little phrases can tell so much about what we really think, feel and experience, how little phrases reveal our deepest convictions. Happy New Year! we say as we kiss our spouse, hug our friends, pet the dog. Happy New Year is so much more than an innocent little phrase. The phrase really expresses our agenda for the New Year.

Happy New Year. We desperately want a happy new year. We're tired of problems. We're tired of our problems; we're tired of our kids' problems. We're tired of the problems at work, within the extended family, within our finances. We're desperately tired of society's problems.

Happy New Year. It's our deepest desire. Happy New Year has an aura of peace, contentment, an undertow of pleasure, rest from the struggles that fill

> our daily lives. Oh, for a year in which all our own personal desires might be
> fulfilled.
>   What we wouldn't give for a Happy New Year!

The move rhetorically explores the sentiment for individualistic, therapeutic relief from the various petty ills that plague us all within American society. It explores the hope for an easier life, a life without disruptions that can grant psychological ease. It works sympathetically with the sentiment—a bit of a danger in light of what is to follow. But the sermon seeks to help the congregation experience the very different ends embedded in the underlying cultural narratives and the underlying biblical narrative.

> *Summary transition.* So much of our lives is wrapped up in such a little phrase,
> Happy New Year. We almost want to close our eyes and dream about it for a little
> while. Happy New Year! Now, I bet I know what you expect; after all, I am a
> preacher. You're all imaging these wonderful scenes of happiness and pleasure,
> vacations on the Caribbean, perfectly adjusted, healthy children, an intimate re-
> lationship with that perfect person. But we're in church. You know I'm sud-
> denly going to say that true happiness can only come through Jesus. You've
> heard it before and you know what's coming now—true self-fulfillment comes
> with faith in God. Relax. I'm not going to say that, because I don't think that
> will help us hear the Scriptures this morning. That just won't help us be formed
> as Christians, friends. No, I want to say something else, something that arises
> from our Scripture reading this morning.

The transition seeks to address the congregation's expectation of a comedic moment, the translation of the biblical text into the normal, cultural experiences of the individual, which they have experienced by years of apologetic preaching. By stating explicitly that there is another interpretation rather than an apologetic approach, the congregation is given rhetorical space, time to prepare for a move in a different direction.

> 2. You see, holiness, not happiness, is God's agenda for our lives. The gospel has
> very little to do with our own personal search for happiness and everything to
> do with God stamping God's own image into our hearts. We were chosen before
> the foundations of the world to be found blameless in love before Jesus Christ.
> This passage from Ephesians is quite remarkable. It comes in the middle of

a doxology, praise to God for the great things God has done. It uses exciting words like *destiny, the purpose of God, the pledge of our inheritance. The mystery of God's will now revealed to us.* Here is the cosmic scope of salvation, the redemption of all that is. This is heady stuff. We typically look at this stuff and poof, it goes right over our heads.

But v. 4 is straightforward. He has chosen us in Christ before the foundations of the world to be holy and blameless before him in love. We have been chosen to be holy. Now, you've been chosen before, right? Remember the days on the playground for kickball? God has chosen you; you have a job to fulfill.

If I read the Scriptures correctly, I don't see that God has chosen you to have a happy New Year—but to be found holy before him in love. We look in vain for any talk of happiness within the passage. Instead, there's the talk of being found holy before him in love. God has an entirely different agenda for our lives than the one that has been taught us by the world. God's plan for our lives involves more than the self-absorbed quest for self-fulfillment that our society calls happiness.

Before anything that is, was, God chose one agenda for human life: to be holy and blameless before him in love.

This entire move explores the different end of human life from that provided by contemporary culture. It is an exercise contrasting the biblical language, upheld by the biblical narrative, from the psychological, therapeutic language given by culture. Resisting translation of the text into individual lives, the move encourages the congregation to embrace the end of life described in the passage.

3. But, John, what is this holy stuff? What does holiness mean? Holiness is nothing less a purity of heart that allows us to stand before God in love. Sanctification is God's cleansing Spirit shaping our very being into the image of Jesus Christ. Our agenda is having the image of God completely restored in our lives by purging the inward sin that clings to our very being.

Let's face it, the word *holy* has a public relations problem today. It needs to hire a political consultant, a spin doctor to help correct its image. When we think of *holy*, we think "sanctimonious," "self-righteousness," you know, the Church Lady played on *Saturday Night Live* reruns. If you wish others a holy new year, they'll think that you are a weird, fanatic, lunatic, fringe cult member.

Friends, holiness is our participation in the very nature of God. God has chosen us to re-create in us the image of love that God has revealed to us in Jesus. Holiness is restoration, the re-formation of our image into the image of God. Holiness is God's righteous love formed in the depths of our beings so that we might love God with all that we are and our neighbors as ourselves.

But face it, we've got a problem. We're fallen creatures. We have this inward

sin that clings to our character like leeches. We didn't ask for it. You can bet
we surely don't choose to show it, but this inward sin mars our lives so. It
brings forth anger, even rage, at those we love. It brings forth insecure feelings that make us want to lash out at those who block our way. We harbor resentment until we're filled with bitterness. This is why holiness involves
cleansing: those sinful patterns, the dispositions that arise not of our choice
but because we participate with a fallen humanity, need to be purged, removed. Holiness is the cleansing of inward sin so that our true nature, the image of God, might be restored that we might love God with all we are and our
neighbor as ourselves.

Holiness isn't about being sanctimonious: it's about being utterly open to
God's grace to cleanse our heart, to reshape our habits to bring forth a character
that reflects God's own holy love.

The language of holiness used here is very traditional Christian language. It is an attempt to go beyond the language of "consecration of
the will as rational self-determination" and "relationship" that dominates
much current discussion of holiness in the Wesleyan-Holiness tradition.
John Wesley was quite content to use such traditional language for holiness. As D. Stephen Long notes:

> In [the sermon] "The Great Privilege" Wesley offers a theological analysis
> of sanctifying human action and its participation in God's infused action.
> He provides a nine-step schematic of human action, infused virtues, and
> the fall into sin. He begins with a term he will use throughout his moral
> theology: the "divine seed" of faith makes it possible for us to participate
> in God's life. Because this is a participation in God's life, it will entail the
> possibility of perfection.[5]

Language of the participation in God helps the congregation to see
themselves in the movement of the biblical narrative of human creation
in God's image, the marring of that image and its restoration through
Jesus Christ, *the* image of God, and the cleansing work of the Holy Spirit.

4. How? How will God fulfill God's intent for our lives? Friends, God brings
forth the image of Jesus in our lives through the body of Christ, the church.
God's holy seed in our hearts matures in us as we live together as the church.
Holiness is no private, individual affair; God's Spirit brings forth God's image in

---

[5]D. Stephen Long, *John Wesley's Moral Theology: The Quest for God and Goodness* (Nashville:
Kingswood, 2005), p. 134.

our lives as we submit to the discipline of the gospel surrounded by those who are on a similar journey.

Did you notice how "we" and "us" and, if we read Greek, "you"(plural) fills this passage? The Scriptures here do not address isolated individuals, each doing their own thing. The Scriptures address the saints, those who have obtained an inheritance, those who were sealed in baptism with the Holy Spirit of promise. It addresses these believers, the church. The Ephesians passage presupposes and demands a concrete, everyday, group of believers. God has chosen us to be holy in the context of other believers, the church.

John Wesley said it this way: " 'Holy private individuals' is a phrase no more consistent with the gospel than holy adulterers. The gospel of Christ knows of no religion, but social; no holiness but social holiness. 'Faith working by love' is the length and breadth and depth and height of Christian perfection." We've forgotten this. The results have been devastating. The church has become some sort of option rather than a means of God's restoring grace. The church has become a place to gather on Sunday mornings, if we have nothing better to do. Our claims to holiness have become emptied of the moral content of God's righteous love. We've learned to live with our inward sin as part of us, excusing it as an essential part of our humanity.

But amid the family united in Jesus, a disciplined community under the lordship of Jesus committed to God's transforming grace, God can and does make a difference. Wesley called it the "social graces." Wesley insisted on regular, consistent corporate worship and the Lord's Supper. But more, he began groups that met together for the pursuit of holiness: the Methodist societies. Small groups gathered weekly for three reasons: mutual encouragement and support, mutual accountability, and visible presence of the church in the society at large. Through these groups Wesley discovered God's grace at work, purifying from inward sin and restoring God's own image of love. We were chosen before the foundations of the world to be holy and blameless before him in love. And if we think this can take place without participation in the body of Christ, the church, I'm afraid that we're kidding ourselves.

God will bring forth God's purpose in our lives as we participate fully, completely, with the saints whom God has called into the journey of the Christian life with us.

Randy Maddox has shown the importance of the Methodist discipline, engaging in the works of mercy and the works of devotion, for Wesley's doctrine of holiness.[6] One could even go so far as to argue that Wesley's thought served to support and internalize the good of pursuing these ec-

[6]See Randy Maddox, *Responsible Grace: John Wesley's Practical Theology* (Nashville: Kingswood, 1994), pp. 192-229.

clesial practices.[7] By joining the doctrine of holiness to particular practices, the sermon makes concrete involvement within the congregation crucial to experiencing the transforming life of God. The doctrine of holiness cannot be privatized but placed within the life of the ecclesial body of Christ.

> *Conclusion.* To be holy and blameless before him in love. This is our agenda for the New Year. In God's image the purpose of our lives becomes aligned with God's purpose. And in the harmony of truth, we may discover the depths of God's grace that may work in human lives through Jesus Christ, our Lord. "Praise be to the God and Father of our Lord Jesus Christ, who has blessed in the heavenly realms with every spiritual blessing in Christ." Amen.

Sermon 3: How May I Be Saved? (Lk 10:25-37)

The parable of the good Samaritan represents a classic text for the moral formation of the church. Within our society the parable is often taken out of the context of dialogue over Torah, a dialogue that presupposes the election of Israel. As a result the text is heard as an "objective, universal, abstract" moral teaching that has nothing to do with ecclesial life but instead calls Christians make society a better place.

The first two sermons engage the covenant of grace and re-place the individual into the biblical narrative as a member of the church. This sermon engages the "federal covenant" in which the Christian individual is called to make society "kinder and gentler." To counter this, the sermon reads the parable in context of the dialogue between the Jewish lawyer and Jesus, and thus, according to the politics of the church, the new Israel. As such, the sermon engages a reading of the text given by Augustine in his important work *De Doctrina Christiana (On Christian Doctrine)*.

The sermon begins with a tragic move, calling forth the political commitments of how the text is usually heard within our culture. It moves to a call for Christian perfection, a perfection characterized by nonviolent love of the enemy. The parable is heard as a much more radical call to the specific witness of the church within the world rather than an individual's attempt to make the world a safer, nicer place to live.

---

[7]See John W. Wright, "Wesley's Theology as Methodist Practice: Postmodern Retrieval of the Wesleyan Tradition," *Wesleyan Theological Journal* 35, no. 2 (2000): 7-31.

Introduction. When was the first time that you heard the parable of the good Samaritan? Christians rightfully tell and retell this parable. Jesus' teaching here is so important for our Christian witness. It's interesting, though, that the parable is part of a larger dialogue, a dialogue important for us to hear. Let's hear the parable in the context of the dialogue between Jesus and the Jewish lawyer. The context is very different from the way we often hear this parable.

1. It's easy for us to hear this text as Americans. When we do, we hear, "Be equally nice to everyone." We're tempted to hear the parable as teaching a kind of a liberal moralism: God does not play favorites; neither should we. We should help poor, disadvantaged folk. We should be helpful, loving and accepting of all no matter their race, creed or color, especially when we find them struck down by the misfortunes of life.

We know this reading; it's the one we teach our kids. Here's this poor Jewish guy, beaten and bloody, by the road. His own people, the self-righteous, educated, bigoted elite walk by in the most undemocratic fashion. It is the Samaritan, of a different race, who stopped to care for the poor guy regardless of his race, creed or color.

From this reading, the message is clear: be nice to unfortunates, even if they are not of your demographic background. Watch out for any claims of the elite and intelligentsia. Search and you can find a common humanity with those who suffer from misfortune. When you come across such people, help them out and the world will be a better place. You can make a difference. You merely have to be nice to the downtrodden.

When we Americans hear the parable of the good Samaritan, the story becomes a story of contributing to the world, making the world more just, by helping out those who can't help themselves.

The tragic move sets up an understanding based on a morality of disinterested obligation, trying to establish a right policy for the congregation to live by at all times. Behind this is a notion of justice that is deeply embedded within the contemporary liberal state. The difference between this notion of justice and the Christian notion, which cannot be separated from the proper worship of God, that has resulted in has prompted Stanley Hauerwas to wonder whether the concept of "justice," as articulated in much contemporary thought, is a bad idea.[8]

Summary transition. Christians are to be nice, helpful people, that's what we hear in this parable. And that's not necessarily wrong. But did you ever notice

---

[8]See Stanley Hauerwas, *After Christendom: How the Church Is to Behave If Freedom, Justice, and a Christian Nation Are Bad Ideas* (Nashville: Abingdon, 1991).

how reading the parable this way divorces it from the dialogue with the Jewish lawyer? What is all this law stuff? Could it be when we hear this text as a moralistic do-goodism that we really can't hear what the text is saying? We have to begin with the initial question in the passage, friends, so that we can hear this parable anew.

The summary looks to the wider text to interrogate the cultural teaching from within. It questions the adequacy of removing the parable from the doctrine of election, which the standard reading rejects. The summary does not remove the congregation's motivation to engage in the works of mercy but seeks to place these actions within a different narrative and political context.

2. The passage begins with an important question: How does one receive eternal life? The lawyer knows the right question: Eternal life can only be given; yet how do we receive it?

Here, a lawyer addresses Jesus. Don't think Perry Mason, or "if the glove doesn't fit, you must acquit." The lawyer is a student of the Torah, a teacher of the Torah, the Jewish law. The lawyer approaches Jesus rabbi to rabbi. His question raises an issue central to the life of the people of God, Israel. The lawyer had read the Old Testament. He knew that Israel, though elect, was not immune from judgment. Sin, idolatry and economic exploitation of God's own people by God's people brought forth judgment. Disobedience to Torah, the law, brought God's judgment. The lawyer knew, as Paul says, that not all Israel is really Israel. Therefore, the question is one of the law: Given that I'm part of God's people, part of God's salvation now, how do I live the law, the Torah, to be among the righteous in the age to come? Given that we're recipients of God's promise now, how can I participate in this promise forever?

The lawyer knew that he didn't choose to be a Jew. It was a gift given to him in God's promise to Abraham. He inherited it. Can you earn an inheritance? No, inheritance comes as a gift. You can't earn an inheritance—but you can lose it. This seems to be the presupposition behind the lawyer's question, rabbi to rabbi, Jew to Jew: How might I live righteously under the law?

He didn't ask, How can I earn eternal life? No, it's a question of Torah, the law given to Israel to make Israel a holy nation, a kingdom of priests for the benefit of the nations. The lawyer asks, How can I be part of the righteous Israel in the age that is to come? How can I be part of the kingdom of God when that kingdom is on earth as it is in heaven? It's an important question: What do individuals need to do now so that they may participate with God for all time as members of God's people.

The discussion of the parable begins with a question: What must I do to inherit eternal life?

By emphasizing the Jewish context of the passage, the move places the text within a narrative of the elect people of God. It seeks to undercut a strong distinction between the life and mission of Jesus and the life and mission of Israel. Learning to understand itself within a common narrative of the Jews, the congregation must see its life in a narrative other than that of individuals trying to make the current society more just.[9]

> 3. The answer is clear: love God with all you are and your neighbor as yourself. The lawyer answers his own question by quoting the Torah, the law that was given to Israel at Sinai: love God and neighbor. The lawyer correctly states what it means to righteously and forever belong to God's people: Love God and neighbor.
>
> Jesus points to the Torah in response to the question. But wait! We're not saved by the law! You're right. We're saved utterly by grace, by the gift, by the inheritance given to us by the Father through the Son in the Holy Spirit. But how do you inherit this life? Jesus points to the law for God's people. The law is not an end in itself, but it forms a people in a distinct way. The law forms the people of God into a holy nation, a kingdom of priests. To be righteous one must be part of a people immersed, shaped and formed by what is written in the law.
>
> Once the lawyer was pointed to the right place, the answer was simple: Love God with all you are; love your neighbor as yourself. Love of God and neighbor are linked together. The lawyer asks, What must I do? Jesus responds, Do this and you will live.
>
> Here is the goal, the end of the life of a member of the people of God, of Israel, of the church as the new Israel. Jesus does not annul or supercede the law. Jesus does not render the law obsolete. Jesus calls members of God's people to the center of the Torah, the means by which they become a holy nation, a kingdom of priests, the means by which their witness to this holy God goes throughout the world. Jesus calls God's people by pointing them to the law's center. The reception, the inheritance of eternal life, to live eternally as part of God's people depends on doing this central thing—loving God with all you are and your neighbor as yourself.
>
> 4. "How might I inherit eternal life?" the lawyer asks. Jesus goes one step further. Don't forget, even your enemy is your neighbor. The one who comes across your path is your neighbor—even if the neighbor is your enemy.

---

[9]For the ecclesiological implications of the Jewish origin of the church, see Gerhard Lohfink, *Does God Need the Church? Toward a Theology of the People of God* (Collegeville, Minn.: Liturgical Press, 1999), and John Howard Yoder, *The Jewish-Christian Schism Revisited,* ed. Michael G. Cartwright and Peter Ochs (Grand Rapids: Eerdmans, 2003).

How can I inherit eternal life? Love God with all you are and your neighbor as yourself. The lawyer wants specifics; he wants the categories well-defined. He agrees with Jesus and now wants to live it out. Then Jesus goes from teaching to meddling. He tells a story. You've all heard it before. This gist of the story, it seems to me, is this Jew gets beaten up, mangled and left to die, and is saved by his enemy, a Samaritan. The hostility between the Samaritans and the Jews is legendary. Go to Luke 9:52-56. Here Samaritans reject Jesus. The disciples respond with a threat of violence. The hate between Samaritan and Jew is very personal. The Jew left to die was the enemy of the Samaritan. Jesus teaches that the enemy is still our neighbor, one to be loved. Love of neighbor actively preserves the life of an enemy.

Hear the moral offense, friends. This is the enemy. There's no appeal to some deeper humanity. Few in the United States would morally fault this Samaritan from walking on by. Hey, we'd understand, maybe even cheer if he picked up a rock and put the Jew out of his misery. We could call it a mercy killing. We know how to treat enemies—we treat enemies with intimidation. If that doesn't work, we treat them with violence and call it justice. We seek to extinguish their lives so they can no longer inflict our lives with pain. But Jesus says it is this neighbor we must love, even when the neighbor is the enemy.

I'm not the first to interpret the passage in this way. Listen to Augustine's *On Christian Doctrine:*

> And who is my neighbor? The Lord told of a certain man who went down from Jerusalem into Jericho and was left injured and almost dead. And He taught that no one was a neighbor except the one who was merciful in healing and caring for the wounded man, putting it in such a way that the questioner himself acknowledged the truth when he was asked. Then Our Lord said to him, "Go and do likewise." Thus we should understand that he is our neighbor to whom the office of mercy should be shown if he needs it, or would be shown it in the event that he did need it. . . . Who does not see that none can be denied the office of mercy when it should be extended even to our enemies? For Our Lord also said, "Love your enemies; do good to them that hate you"; . . . it is manifest that every person is to be thought of as a neighbor, for evil must be committed toward no one.

> Do this and you will live; go and do likewise: love God with all you are and your neighbor as yourself. And your enemy, the person who hates you, is your neighbor.

The move contrasts the disembodied ethic with the ethic coming out of the doctrine of election and the teachings of Jesus on nonretaliation and nonviolent love for the enemy. Rather than a teaching to help society function better, the sermon now allows the parable to form a people whose love of their enemies contrasts with the legitimated violence of the nation. By quoting Augustine, the father of Christian just-war theory, the interpretation of the passage, seemingly radical and different, is seen within the interpretive tradition of a different polity, the church. The sermon enjoins the congregation to see themselves as a much broader, much more inclusive people than members of the contemporary nation.

> *Conclusion.* How might I inherit eternal life? What does the law say? Love God and your neighbor, even your enemy. In the life of Jesus, especially on the cross, we see the law fulfilled. Jesus loved God and neighbor, even his enemy, even you, even me. The law as seen in Jesus demands we preserve our enemies' lives, not to respond with vengeance. Our reception of eternal life, our witness as a holy people, a kingdom of priests, hinges on the mercy, not the violence, we show our enemies. And so we turn to this Table. Here we discover that even though we are sinners, enemies of God, we are guests at the Lord's Table. Come in faith. Come out of love of God and love of neighbor. Come, so that you might inherit eternal life. Come, and be thankful.

Sermon 4. There *Is* a King in Israel (Judg 21:15-25; Lk 2:10-12)

This sermon differs from the previous three in several ways. Most obviously, the sermon arises out of an Old Testament text. The sermon originated within a class, "The Beginnings of the Hebrew Nation," rather than within a specific congregation. I did not choose the text—the class assigned it to me to illustrate a typological reading of the Old Testament for the benefit of the church. And they chose one of the most difficult texts in all of the Scriptures! Since it was the end of the fall semester, we were within the Advent season. The context of the liturgical year of the church opened the text to a new hearing.

The sermon differs as well from the earlier sermons in its basic relationship with the biblical text. This sermon, based within an extended narrative, adopts a more directly narrative means of explication. The congregation is interwoven directly into the biblical text in the sermon. The tragic moves function differently by identifying the congregation with Israel at one of their lowest points in the biblical story. The congregation, dealing with stresses that arise out of the commercialization of the Christmas season, becomes Israel in the moment of their deepest debauchery—not necessarily a flattering comparison. This permits, however, the proclamation of the good news: in the birth of the Messiah, God has empowered God's people to live faithfully in the world. Life as the messianic people of God makes possible a different shaping of our desires. We can move away from the consumerist desires embedded within us by Christmas—and its subsequent moral difficulties.[10] In order to highlight the narrative flow of the sermon, it will be given uninterrupted by additional comments.

Introduction. We like warm, cozy Christmas images. Chestnuts roasting on fires. Dreaming of a white Christmas. Snow gently falling. In North America, images of Christmas make us want to get out a comforter or snuggle with someone special in front of a gentle fire. Then there's this passage from Judges. It's gross, slimy, vile. It makes us uncomfortable. It's not in the Christmas spirit at all. But I wonder. Maybe only as we confront the reality of Judges 21 can we really experience the good news of the birth of the Messiah, Jesus Christ.

1. Judges 21 reveals how life had unwound for Israel. It's ugly. Plug the kids' ears; the story sounds like something from a back alley in L.A. Despite God's faithfulness, Israel had fallen apart.

We read the end of a story that runs from Judges 19—21. The whole thing starts with a Levite and a concubine having a falling out, a domestic fight. Reconciliation happens. Yet on the way home, horror strikes. The couple stops among the Benjaminites, a tribe of Israel, for a night's lodging. The townsfolk show up at the house, wanting sexual favors from their guest. The Levite gives them his concubine, and the townsfolk rape her throughout the night. She is found on the doorstep in the morning. Then, if possible, the story gets worse. The Levite hacks her body into pieces, and sends it to the other tribes within Israel. Now war breaks out, civil war. Israel is unwinding. What began as a domestic spat takes all of Israel to the brink of utter chaos.

Barbarians. Really? You know how little things build; before we know it, chaos gathers steam. We're all up in arms against Benjamin. Life literally starts unwinding around us.

"Well, at least I'm not that way." Again, I wonder. Hopefully we're not cutting bodies up in the garage. But have you ever noticed how sin swirls in our lives? Even little domestic spats grow, relentlessly digging its claws into us, drawing us deeper, deeper into conflict. We try to hide it during the holiday season. We smile, but we feel it underneath, growing, growing until it suddenly explodes.

It's ugly. Here's Israel, the elect of God, engaging in rape, dismemberment, war. Life had just unwound for Israel.

---

[10]For life within the church as an alternative technology of desire to contemporary neoliberal capitalism, see Daniel M. Bell, *Liberation Theology at the End of History: The Refusal to Cease Suffering* (London: Routledge, 2001).

2. And so, here we are, standing on the brink of our own self-annihilation. We're caught with the consequences of our sin, and the gravity of the situation smacks us in the face. Suddenly we realize that we're about to bring about our own extinction.

What is it about the "holiday season" in this society? We have a goal—live until Christmas Eve with our lives, our bodies, our emotions, our relationships intact. It gets nasty out there, downright nasty. The rush, tumble, bump and grind. Emotions get pent up; feelings build. Suddenly they're out in the open, raw, savage, cruel. Emotions, vices spring up from nowhere. All of a sudden we look at ourselves and can't believe it. What have we done? We recognize we're caught in patterns that destroy everything that we hold dear.

That's where Israel is in this text. It's brutal, absolutely brutal. Then someone wakes up. Wait a second. Should we annihilate Benjamin? They're one of us. The chain of violence is not taking Israel anywhere except for the extermination of one of their own. The Scriptures say that the people had compassion on them (Judg 21:15). Benjamin has been brought to the edge of extinction. There, Israel is hit with the awareness of the stupidity, the sinfulness, the futility of the whole cycle. They can no longer afford to deny the consequences. They stop right on the edge of utter futility.

We can only deny the implications of our behavior, the cycles of vengeance that we seek, for so long. We sense life slipping away from us, and we recognize we have to do something about it. Maybe it's not too late.

That's the way it is so often. Pulled in by a cycle of our own self-destruction, it's like a slap in the face. We wake up, hopefully, before it's too late.

3. What a mess! What's Israel to do? Standing on the edge of destruction, what options do they have? They've painted themselves in a corner. What now? Quite simply, the Benjaminites grabbed what was available. Self-preservation was at stake; Benjamin found a way to deal with the situation without really dealing with the problem. Benjamin continued to exist by avoiding changing anything, suppressing the rupture caused by their sin, yet living to see another day.

Hey, what's the problem? The conflict is stopped. Just kiss and make up. Let everyone go their own merry way. But it's not that simple, is it? It never is. The Israelites had made vows. They had conspired together to wipe out Benjamin. Now they have to deal with the consequences. What to do? The tribe of Benjamin needs babies, Israelite babies born to Israelite women. Yet the Israelites can't give their daughters in marriage to the Benjaminites because of the vow they made earlier.

One has to admire their ingenuity. There's a big festival at Shiloh. Young Israelite women are there dancing. Vineyards surround the area. The Benjaminites hide, grab the women and take them for wives. If you won't give us your daughters, we'll take them. There is no consent. They need children. They grab the young women, go home and impregnate them. They don't need consent; they need babies. They find what's at hand and use it. Ironically, it's the same behavior that started the whole mess, grabbing a young woman for their own sexual use.

It's horrible, horrible. It gives us the creeps. But wait a second. How different are they from us? When our back's against the wall, caught by our cycles of sin, we want to survive. We grab what's at hand and get through the moment. We'll survive and deal with the consequences later. Maybe we'll even do what got us in trouble in the first place. We don't care. That's not the issue. Survival matters. We try to pull our world back from the edge.

That's where Benjamin was. They grabbed the dancing women to get themselves out of a fix.

4. It just doesn't seem right, does it? Not then. Not now. Somehow it seems that they missed the point; they never address the problem. What is the problem? There is no moral center. There's nothing to rule within but our own selves, our own unchecked desires, our own perpetual Christmas lists. We try to survive by doing whatever we have to do. Survival becomes an end in itself—we do what is right in our own eyes.

The passage has a haunting end. "In these days, Israel had no king; everyone did as he saw fit" (v. 25). We want hope that the story will resolve itself. They settle the issue for now, but, on the other hand, the Benjaminites don't solve anything. There is no king in Israel. Grab a dancing woman, whatever. Just do it. Follow your uncheck desires to where they end.

There is no king in Israel; every person did what was right in their own eyes. We are so there. The world shapes our lives into cycles that eventually collapse inward; we are on the edge and so we grab whatever is available just to survive. We get by. Isn't that what Christmas is all about? We deny the destructive forces in our lives, bury memories in presents, smile at family functions. Yet the darkness still looms. There is no center, only void. We try to find the center in the latest TV commercials; we do what's right in our own eyes. If it means grabbing a dancing woman from Shiloh, let's get at it.

You see, we've been formed by a society that tells us what matters is our own self-interest, our own consumption, our own unchecked desires, desires formed within us by those who profit most from them. There is no king in Israel; every person did what they see fit. We even have a holiday to keep consumption up—we call it Christmas. We'll worry about the bills later; right now we have to survive—we have to pursue our own interests. We deny any real solution and grab what's at hand to survive. We live without any moral check on ourselves.

Even Christmas can't help. When there is no moral center, no king in Israel, the only thing to do, other than utterly giving up, is to do what's right in our own eyes. Yet that only continues the problem, the destructive cycles in which our lives have become embedded.

Transition summary. There was no king in Israel; every person did what was right in their own eyes. Well, merry Christmas. Can we dare to be honest? Dare we confront the vacuous despair that haunts our lives, which we do our best to deny? Dare we identify ourselves with the sons of Benjamin, grabbing the young women, not thinking about the problems it's going to cause us in the New Year? Is there no king in Israel this Christmas season?

5. Friends, I've got good news for you—there is a king in Israel. For unto us is born this day in the city of David, a Savior who is Christ, Messiah, King of Israel. Glory to God in the highest; on earth peace, good will to all people. The King has come!

Can you hear the thrill of the angels' message to the shepherds? "Do not be afraid. I bring you good news of great joy that will be for all the people" (Lk 2:10-11). There is a king in Israel! The center has come! We're not going to find the center within; we're not doing what comes naturally. God has intervened—the center is outside us. The center is Jesus Christ. Wonderful, Counselor, the Everlasting Father, the Prince of Peace. A baby, lying in a manger. He is the king of Israel, the Son of David. Because of Christmas, there is and always will be a king in Israel forevermore!

Do you get what this means? We no longer have to grab whatever works. No longer do we have to live competing for our own self-interests, doing what is right in our own eyes. No longer do we have to live in denial, caught in downward spirals of sin, doing our best just to survive. No! God has become human and dwelled among us, and we have beheld his glory, the glory of the Father's only Son, full of grace and truth! God entered the cycles of Israel's life in Jesus Christ and called us into God's people through him! God has provided the center for all humanity in Jesus, the King. And we find the moral center of our lives only as we live under his rule, in his kingdom. Our desires do not have to be shaped by the market around us. In him we find a way past grabbing the dancing young women so that our lives are worth living, our desires are shaped by the kingdom that has come in the body of the King. For in Jesus, God has provided the Messiah, the King in Israel.

When Jesus Christ entered the world, everything changed. By confessing his rule, his kingship, his lordship, we are given a center along with his people, his kingdom. He provides a center outside ourselves that provides the mooring when we feel the cycles that threaten to overwhelm us coming. There's a center to life. He provides a center to return to, and this center holds. He teaches us our true desires. Among his people, there is a center to break the spirals, the horrible tendency we have to grab whatever we think we can use. God has sent the Messiah, his Son, Jesus Christ into the world!

We no longer have to fend for ourself. Hear the good news: There is a king in Israel.

Conclusion. Christmas isn't about trying to pull it together for a few days a year when all our self-interests are served simultaneously. Christmas isn't about a sentimental time that helps us to deny the cold, hard reality about our lives. Christmas is not about some abstract principle of love that briefly overtakes us when our lives are spiraling out of control. And it's definitely not about grab-

> bing some dancing women to help our own survival. Christmas proclaims that
> there is a king in Israel, Jesus Christ. God's kingdom has come near in him.
> "Glory to God in the highest, and on earth peace to all persons on whom God's
> favor rests!"

Conclusion

These four sermons attempt to illustrate a homiletic of turning that
moves a congregation from narrative horizons of the culture into the biblical narrative governed by the distinct, peculiar politics of the church.
The sermons attempt to refocus human lives by placing them as characters within God's story rather than putting God into stories of the individual or the nation. As such, they embrace a tragic moment, a moment
of difference when the biblical text reads the congregation. They attempt
to recover the distinctive theological importance of the church for the
Christian formation of the individual and as the primary locus of witness
to the God revealed in Jesus Christ.

Yet homiletics is only one means for the conversion and sanctification
of a congregation. A homiletics of turning must have a context within
other practices of a congregation, both to be heard and to maintain its
moral credibility. Pastoral care and leadership, therefore, can never be
limited to preaching or oversight of the church's programming.

Embracing a homiletic of turning also requires an understanding of
how the culture has provided the horizons for much contemporary pastoral practice. Alternative ecclesial practices, arising out of the Christian
Scriptures, not only support a homiletic of turning but also give the final
rationale for why it is important. Given the risk of swimming upstream,
chapter five will place the homiletic of this book into a broader pattern
of pastoral care and congregational practices.

Weaving the Story and the Rhetoric of Pastoral Care

Convictions form the lives of individuals and groups, and they usually function unconsciously. Profound trauma can accompany exposing, calling into question and shifting convictions. Tragedy, after all, is tragedy. When planes slammed into the World Trade Center on September 11, 2001, the immediate tragedy of the moment reverberated throughout the United States and other nations. Americans realized that they were not immune from the violence that continually shakes much of the world.

Citizens of the United States suddenly discovered that they were vulnerable to attack, even at home. Events forced people to see what had always been true but had been obscured by a narrative of invulnerability. As events exploded this narrative, governmental officials tried to restore the confidence in the old narrative of invulnerability by developing new practices of surveillance and aggression. Yet a new sense of anxiety accompanied life, an anxiety that arose from a shift of convictions. Despite the government's continued soteriological language, the new practices have not been fully effective; indeed we could even argue that some practices have proved counterproductive. Anxiety remains.

Weaving individuals into the biblical narrative as individual yet corporate actors takes historical and cultural awareness, theological acumen, and technical homiletic skill. We have focused on these in the first four chapters. While these distinct skills are necessary, they are not sufficient in and of themselves for faithfully weaving congregations into the biblical narrative.

It takes more. If we are to narrate the story of God to form a people into a distinct, peculiar community, specific rhetorical skills are required. This rhetoric must go beyond the structuring of a sermon. Unless a congregation embodies the biblical narrative through particular practices while avoiding others, the rhetoric will remain merely that—verbiage that does not form but only obscures a congregation's true commitments. The *practices* of a local congregation provide the rhetorical background through which the Spirit might form and sustain a peculiar people whose visible witness provides the world with alternatives that it otherwise would not have known were possible.

Pastoral practices must then reinforce congregational practices. Within North American culture, pastoral practices must initiate and support individuals through the trauma of narrative transformation. Even more, the pastor must support the congregation through the ongoing individual and corporate adjustments that arise when they live with convictions that differ with the world's. To speak in terms of the Christian tradition, the pastor must commit to the congregation's sanctification.

In this chapter I will examine the governing therapeutic pastoral rhetoric of contemporary North American culture. I do not reject this rhetoric but seek to place the inevitable therapeutic dimensions of the contemporary pastorate into a different narrative framework. Freeing genuinely Christian therapeutic concerns from their captivity to North American culture, I will speak of the pastor as a beginning place for an embodiment of a rhetoric to form a congregation into a kingdom of priests, a holy nation.

Preaching and the Therapeutic Pastorate

Many pastors would readily agree that the pastorate is more difficult today than ever before in its North American setting. Anecdotes and statistics tell the same story: burnout, moral failure, high stress, fall-out on families, financial strain. The list goes on and on. Dysfunctional dynamics within congregations, a competitive marketplace for recruiting and maintaining members, and an increasing number of people who see the clergy as unreliable combine to challenge those who answer God's call. Within the vocation itself the required competencies continue to mount: leader, administrator, public speaker, psychologist, building manager, social worker, personnel director, crisis counselor, vision director, fundraiser. Again, the list goes on and on. To maintain competency in two or three areas commonly demanded of pastors would be remarkable; competency in all of expectations is ludicrous. The pastorate seems more difficult today because it *is* more difficult.

Given such circumstances, it is easy to understand why pastors engage in a comedic translation of the biblical text for congregational consumption. Christians expect sermons to supplement their personal lives, sermons that will draw them back the next week for one more Sunday treatment—and maybe even bring a friend. Why complicate things by confronting them with a tragic moment? The job is difficult enough as it is! Why risk alienating the faithful? Why hamper the church's ability to compete in the local religious marketplace for the migratory consumers who might stop by and try out a service?

A comedic pastoral rhetoric, however, may actually create the very problem it is meant to solve.[1] To understand the rhetorical context for pastoral practice, it again is helpful to return to the cultural and historical horizons in which many North Americans live. Here the anthropological work of Robert Bellah and his team may help us to understand the conundrum pastors find themselves in so that a way out might be offered.[2]

As mentioned in chapter one, contemporary culture divides life into two distinct spheres: the public and the private, or the managerial and therapeutic realms. These realms have distinctive purposes. The public, managerial realm seeks efficiency in a competitive economic marketplace. The managerial realm is the realm of the workplace, of government, of politics. Here the individual must do whatever it takes to keep her or his organization competitive in the marketplace. In the managerial realm the individual seeks "to persuade, inspire, manipulate, cajole, and intimidate

---

[1]Philip Cushman, a psychotherapist, argues the same for decontextualized approaches to psychotherapy: "approaches that imply that therapy is a healing technology that transcends the politics and culture of its era . . . fail because they promise the impossible. . . . They cannot free themselves to comment directly on the structural causes of local emotional ills, grasp their unintended involvement in the perpetuation of those ills, or devise therapeutic practices that would attempt to heal those ills without simultaneously reproducing them. Most object relations, humanistic, cognitive, and addiction therapies, for instance, however effective in producing behavior change or emotional experiences in the short run, inevitably reproduce the very causes of the ills they treat by implicitly valorizing and reproducing the isolated, empty individual" (*Constructing the Self, Constructing America: A Cultural History of Psychotherapy* [Boston: Addison-Wesley, 1995], p. 7).

[2]See chap. 1.

those he manages so that his organization measures up to criteria of effectiveness shaped ultimately by the market but specifically by the expectations of those in control of his organization—finally, its owners."[3]

The managerial realm is supposedly principled, abstract, rational, disembodied. Those within it must often operate impersonally in light of
the broader competitive economic realities. Individuals receive financial
compensation in response to the maximum value that they can negotiate
for their productivity. In North American society, such a realm has a distinctly male-gendered cast to it.[4] People win in this realm by competing
with their peers for the opportunity to move up the ladder of managerial
responsibility, and thus receive more economic compensation. Of
course, such a fierce, competitive realm takes a toll on individuals. A
slow psychological drain accompanies the constant strife within the
managerial realm for winners and losers alike.

Another realm must accompany such a dog-eat-dog sphere of life in
order to sustain such basic activities as child-rearing and basic human
cooperation. Thus the culture generates a private, therapeutic realm to
help compensate for the competitiveness of the public realm. The private, therapeutic realm provides personal affirmation, meaning, self-
fulfillment and expression—what has come recently to be called "spirituality."[5] The private, therapeutic realm is the realm of relationships,
family, leisure, intimacy and sexuality. In the therapeutic realm the person must achieve psychological equilibrium, emotional solace, comfort
and personal happiness. Therapists, formal and informal, must arise to
meet the needs produced by the managerial realm. "Like the manager,
the therapist is a specialist in mobilizing resources for effective action,
only here the resources are largely internal to the individual and the
measure of effectiveness is the elusive criterion of personal satisfaction."[6]

The therapeutic sphere is relational, concrete, communicative and

---

[3]Robert Bellah et al., *Habits of the Heart : Individualism and Commitment in American Life*
(Berkeley: University of California Press, 1996), p. 45; and Dorothy Smith, *The Everyday World
as Problematic: A Feminist Sociology* (Boston: Northeastern University Press, 1987).

[4]See Smith, *The Everyday World as Problematic*.

[5]For an excellent analysis of how the rise of the language of "spirituality" extends the commod-
ification of historical traditions for the consumption of the individual consumer as part of a
neoliberal economic program, see Jeremy Carrette and Richard King, *Selling Spirituality: The
Silent Takeover of Religion* (London: Routledge, 2004).

[6]Bellah, *Habits of the Heart*, p. 47.

embodied. It always operates personally in light of the specific needs of an individual as he or she copes with the struggles of his or her own concrete history. In general, it has a distinctly female-gendered cast to it and offers little if any of the public affirmation or financial compensation provided by the managerial realm. One wins in the therapeutic realm by curing the disjunction between the present organization of the self and the available organization of work, intimacy, and meaning. And this cure takes the form of enhancing and empowering the self to be able to relate successfully to others in society, achieving a kind of satisfaction without being overwhelmed by their demands. In its own understanding, the expressive aspect of our culture exists for the liberation and fulfillment of the individual.[7] *Balance* becomes a key virtue for sustaining life within such a cultural arrangement.

Bellah argues that contemporary culture isolates the managerial from the therapeutic in ways that did not exist earlier in history.[8] Most of us no longer work, for instance, on a family farm where the parson drops in for pie just before the family engages in their evening chores. The contemporary differentiation between the public and the private should not, however, obscure the interrelationship between the managerial and therapeutic realms.

In one sense the managerial realm exists for the sake of the therapeutic. We seek to achieve success in the managerial realm in order to produce economic resources for higher levels of enjoyment and freedom in the therapeutic realm. Success in the managerial realm enables financial resources for more therapeutic opportunities for our family and ourself. As the saying goes, "the one who dies with the most toys wins."

Yet in a deeper sense the therapeutic realm exists for the sake of the

---

[7]Ibid.

[8]"America was colonized by those who had come loose from the older European structures, and so from the beginning we had a head start in the process of modernization. Yet the colonists brought with them ideas of social obligation and group formation that disposed them to recreate in America structures of family, church, and polity that would continue, if in modified form, the texture of older European society. Only gradually did it become clear that every social obligation was vulnerable, every tie between individuals fragile. Only gradually did what we have called ontological individualism, the idea that the individual is the only firm reality, become widespread. Even in our day, when separation and individuation have reached a kind of culmination, their triumph is far from complete. The battles of modernity are still being fought" (ibid., p. 276).

managerial. As the managerial realm extracts a personal toll, the therapeutic exists to compensate for the personal turmoil caused by the managerial. Therapy, formal or informal, empowers the individual to enter and reenter the managerial fray like a soldier returning to the battlefield after a three-day leave. Competition and pressure increase with more responsibility within the managerial sphere. Thus the more one succeeds managerially, the more one needs the therapeutic to deal with the pressure. As Bellah writes, "Domesticality, love, and intimacy increasingly became 'havens' against the competitive culture of work."[9]

Such therapy, however, takes more financial resources, which again, sends one back to produce more financial resources for the meaningful activities of the therapeutic realm. The two realms thus relate in a production-consumption cycle that upholds the economic system. One produces to consume and consumes to produce.

The individual must constantly negotiate between the managerial and therapeutic realms. These negotiations weigh heavily upon us because no moral basis for appropriate adjudication exists outside the individual self. Finding the right balance becomes a matter of a consumer's choice and personal satisfaction:

> What is good is what one finds rewarding. If one's preferences change, so does the nature of the good. Even the deepest ethical virtues are justified as matters of personal preference. Indeed, the ultimate ethical rule is simply that individuals should be able to pursue whatever they find rewarding, constrained only by the requirement that they not interfere with the "value systems" of others.[10]

The result is what Alasdair MacIntyre calls "emotivism," "the doctrine that all evaluative judgments and more specifically all moral judgments are *nothing but* expressions of preference, expressions of attitude or feeling, insofar as they are moral or evaluative in character."[11] Like standing in front of eight brands of sliced peaches in the grocery store, one can easily experience overload by the sheer volume and irrationality of the choices.

---

[9] Ibid., p. 43.
[10] Ibid., p. 6.
[11] Alasdair MacIntyre, *After Virtue,* 2nd ed. (Notre Dame, Ind.: University of Notre Dame Press, 1984), pp. 11-12.

All life becomes commodified; commitment to any community for any other reason than perceived self-interest is eroded. Ultimately, "American cultural traditions define personality, achievement, and the purpose of human life in ways that leave the individual suspended in glorious, but terrifying, isolation."[12] The culture produces persons that demand therapy for affirmation amid continual decisions that they must make, when the decisions themselves are made with no greater goal than a person's own fulfillment.

These cultural contours are inescapable for the contemporary church. Though strictly a social construct and in no way natural, such life experiences surround and pervade us as much as the air we breathe. Whether the church embraces this context or develops into a peculiar people that discerns where and how to be different makes all the difference in the world.

The contemporary plight of the pastor originates within the assimilative patterns that the church in North America has taken in both its liberal and conservative forms. Assimilating to its cultural context, the church exists as an institution to purvey the generalized experience of religion. Religion itself has become a personal matter, strictly belonging to the private, therapeutic realm. In this context, churches exist to help individuals find meaning and fulfillment in an otherwise competitive environment. Churches exist as therapeutic safe houses in an impersonal world.[13]

The assimilative church carves out a therapeutic niche for those

---

[12]Bellah, *Habits of the Heart*, p. 6.

[13]"The reason for describing them as 'safe houses' is that an enculturated church has no other identity to distinguish it from its cultural context. . . . [T]he enculturated congregation has to draw a clear line between itself and the rest of the world precisely because it reflects so much of the world. Its only recourse is to see itself as a place where the best of worldly values can be found—only more abundantly. This stance will often require it to reach out into the community; but from the safe house perspective, the purpose of this outreach is almost always to invite friends, neighbors and others to share the blessings its members already enjoy.

"The identity of safehouse congregations lies in viewing their discipleship and their community life as sources of maximum personal benefit—a perspective that increasingly leads to alienation from those who do not share these blessings with them. To the extent that this identity shapes their day-to-day relationships, they see themselves as different from everyone else, and out of place in a world where they do not belong" (David Lowes Watson, *Forming Christian Disciples: The Role of Covenant Discipleship and Class Leaders in the Congregation*, rev. ed. [Nashville: Discipleship Resources, 1995], p. 28).

wounded by the managerial world in order to find healing and hope with a personal relationship with God and fellowship with other like-minded, similarly needy individuals. This church reinforces the culture by binding its wounded and sending them back to the front to rejoin the consumption-production cycle. The assimilative church empowers individuals to find the proper balance as the individual negotiates his or her way within the consumerist cycle. Commitment to the church, therefore, arises from the individual needs that the church meets. As Bellah writes, "Community and attachment come not from the demands of a tradition, but from the empathetic sharing of feelings among therapeutically attuned selves."[14] Commitment to God becomes a commitment to the fulfilled self.

Personal needs lie at the center of the church's life in the assimilative church. Congregations face tremendous pressures to have their own needs met and to reach out to meet the needs of others for recruitment purposes. A congregation must compete with other churches in its vicinity to maintain membership and attract new members. If unending demands do not exhaust the institution and its personnel, the market pressures themselves can undermine the ongoing vitality of the church. "The salience of these needs for personal intimacy in American religious life suggests why the local church, like other voluntary communities, indeed like the contemporary family, is so fragile, requires so much energy to keep it going, and has so faint a hold on commitment when such needs are not met."[15]

Given such a cultural context, the assimilative church needs a special type of leader. The assimilative church requires a personally therapeutic pastor who, nonetheless, has the managerial skills necessary to run the church as a therapeutic service agency. The range of expertise this takes is astounding. The pastor has to meet the therapeutic needs of individuals while overseeing the whole organization. There is no communal good outside of the individual that the pastor seeks to serve, except perhaps to ensure the smooth operation of the society that is producing the dysfunction in the first place. Service to God is translated into meeting

---

[14]Bellah, *Habits of the Heart*, p. 232.
[15]Ibid.

the needs of the demographic market segment that the church represents as each individual attempts to negotiate his or her way through the
public and private realms.

Of course, pastors face the same therapeutic demands that each member of the congregation experiences. Yet pastors often have no pastoral
therapeutic outlet for their own needs. Constantly giving of their own
self, often with minimal financial resources or leisure time to recover,
faced with criticism for real or perceived lack of therapeutic or managerial skills, the therapeutic pastorate is not very therapeutic for those who
attempt to fill its office. Pastors of larger churches, those who have sufficient financial resources to disperse the congregational expectations to
various specialized staff, an office staff to protect them from the drain of
the constant demands, and sufficient material comforts, can survive,
even thrive, within such an assimilative context. Pastors of typical congregations, however, find the task much more daunting, even defeating.
The demands are too intense and unending.

The assimilative church demands a certain kind of homiletical rhetoric. The society shapes a congregation to look to religion for help in ne-
gotiating a way to find personal fulfillment. Sermons are a central practice for the assimilative church to achieve such an end. Individuals
gather together for weekly encouragement and equipment. Homiletical
rhetoric, therefore, has developed to help individuals cope with negoti-
ating the balance between the managerial and the therapeutic. Pastors
craft sermons to meet the societal demand that has been taught to old,
new and potential parishioners: to enable the individual to find the inner
strength (i.e., faith) to overcome obstacles for a meaningful personal life
through a personal (i.e., therapeutic) relationship with God. Theological
versions of therapeutic language provide the content for most contemporary sermons.

American Christianity has provided a resource for the development of
such a therapeutic homiletical rhetoric. The Puritans built their regular
sermon around the covenant of grace, in which an individual moves
from a negative state (sin) to a positive state (salvation) by the grace of
God in Jesus Christ. This narrative can undergo simple modification
without disturbing its fundamental structure. All that needs to be done
is to translate the terms of these states into contemporary therapeutic

language. The negative state (sin) can easily become individual feelings of alienation, and the positive state (salvation) translates easily into an expressivist language of self-fulfillment. Rather than grace as the forgiveness of sin, God's grace becomes God's empowering presence in a personal relationship that helps individuals overcome the experiences of disquiet that come from living in the culture.

Having received this inner experience of assurance of divine love, the pastor guides the church to live a good, balanced, fulfilled life within the society. Psychological, expressivist themes replace biblical and theological terms. The church's language becomes that of a support group to help people overcome personal obstacles.

Preachers have developed a homiletical rhetoric of therapy to help them deal with the needs of their parishioners. By meeting their needs in the sermon, it is hoped that the parishioners may survive the week as relatively well-adjusted, autonomous individuals. Perhaps they can even contribute to meeting the needs of others, thus lightening the load on the pastor!

Yet rather than solving the problems that contemporary pastors face, such a pastoral rhetoric ends up sustaining precisely the problems that it is meant to solve. The therapeutic rhetoric calls for the pastor to be the CEO of a helping organization. The pastor becomes entrapped within the rhetoric provided by the culture. The rhetoric can only momentarily pause the pattern of need. The unending cycle of moving between the therapeutic and managerial realms creates more need for pastoral reassurance.

A Pauline Alternative to the Therapeutic Pastorate

To escape the excessive demands of the therapeutic pastorate, we have to develop an alternate rhetoric to that given by the culture. We must develop specific Christian language that presents the church as a visible manifestation of the redemptive presence of God.

Obviously, reshaping a congregation's life by the biblical narrative is not therapeutic. The biblical narrative does not tell us how to negotiate between public and private realms, nor how an individual might live a meaningful, self-fulfilled life. These simply are not categories consistent with the biblical narrative. The biblical narrative reveals how individuals might become members of God's elect people in order to witness to God's love, a witness that can—and often does—involved suffering for righteousness's sake.

Yet, formed faithfully, the ecclesial witness *does* provide a therapeutic function—in the unity and mutuality of a local congregation that lives amid the potential hostility of an unredeemed world. The witness of the church demands that it be formed into a people whose relations with each other provide the therapeutic dimensions necessary to live faithfully for God in a hostile world.

Such an expectation is evident in Philippians 1. At the end of the chapter, Paul, in chains because of the gospel of Christ, tells the congregation: "For it has been granted to you on behalf of Christ not only to believe on him, but also to suffer for him, since you are going through the same struggle you saw I had, and now hear that I still have" (Phil 1:29-30). Paul saw that faith in Christ brought suffering, not therapeutic self-fulfillment. Loyalty to the gospel and the Christian formation of the church had set Paul at odds with the authorities around him.

Paul knew that his arrest also put the church in Philippi at risk. As a powerless minority in the society, they too could end up the target of hostility because of their peculiar friendship with Paul. This is the price that the Philippian church might pay—and were paying—for their nonconformity to the society around them as a result of their allegiance to Christ.

Such passages like Philippians 1:27-30 are not preached much these days. They do not give us four steps out of personal depression or information on how to experience God's presence at the low tide of life. They have nothing to say about "be happy attitudes." Yet the suffering that Paul describes is not without a support system—the bodies of other believers within the local, and universal, church.

Paul exhorts the Philippians in 2:1-4 to respond to the threat of persecution by solidarity with each other.[16] Because of the nature of the Spirit's presence, this solidarity can be described in therapeutic terms. Paul writes:

---

[16]Stephen E. Fowl, *Philippians,* Two Horizons New Testament Commentary (Grand Rapids: Eerdmans, 2005), pp. 77-88.

> If you have encouragement from being united with Christ, if any comfort
> from his love, if any fellowship with the Spirit, if any tenderness and com-
> passion, then make my joy complete by being like-minded, having the
> same love, being one in spirit and purpose. Do nothing out of selfish am-
> bition or vain conceit, but in humility consider others better than your-
> selves. Each of you should look not only to your own interests, but also
> to the interests of others. (Phil 2:1-4)

Paul envisions the Philippians coming together amid the hostility of a
society that possesses different allegiances and therefore different practices and virtues. The whole passage, both its suffering and solidarity,
has a Christological basis. Stephen Fowl observes, "Paul's point here
would seem to be that the bonds of love uniting the Philippians (and
Paul) in Christ are the basis for comfort in the midst of suffering. The
character of that love and by implication the quality of the comfort it provides are shaped, determined and manifested by Christ."[17]

Together in Christ, God brings forth sustaining, enriching, healing ties
that empower each believer within the context of the whole Christian
community, the church. The church's therapeutic function arises out of
the faithfulness of its witness; it does not replace or define that witness.
To do so is to sentimentalize the gospel, holding it captive to the emotional needs of individuals within a congregation. The solidarity of affections sustains the church in order to maintain a faithfulness of life amid
pressure to assimilate to the world.

Within God's story the church does not aim to provide therapeutic
services for disturbed individuals. The church does not exist so that individuals might seek intimacy with others, themselves or God. The
church exists as a people, a distinct people, whose witness can bring opposition from the world through the fact of its nonconformity, but whose
communal life provides concrete, embodied resources for support amid
the resultant suffering.

If this is so, ironically, the most therapeutic function that the pastor
may undertake is to form the church as the church, a peculiar people,
in the world through its unique witness. This shifts the role of the pastor.
No longer a therapeutic specialist with managerial skills to run a service

---

[17]Ibid., p. 80.

organization, the pastor must help a congregation "live as a colony of resident aliens within a hostile environment, which, in the most subtle but deadly ways, corrupts and coopts us as Christians."[18] The pastor's job is to keep the church unified in its faithful witness in the world. When the pastor seeks to form a congregation within the biblical narrative, "the pastor is called to help us gather the resources we need to be the colony of God's righteousness."[19]

This task paints an entirely different landscape for the pastor. The pastor exercises her or his gifts within the church, a people who understands that it is necessary for it to have one mind, the mind of Christ. This is how Paul engaged his pastoral task to the Philippian church, even when separated by geography and chains. Paul

> has offered the Philippians an account of their situation in the light of God's economy. As they find themselves in the same struggle that he is in, graced not only with faith, but the opportunity of suffering for Christ's sake, he encourages them to act in ways analogous to the ways he has acted. He urges them (and us) to form their desires and plans and their common life in such a way that they will be able to continue, like him, to live in a manner worthy of the gospel. The central virtue which will enable this sort of common life is the formation of a common perspective, a common pattern of thinking and acting which will enable them to understand rightly their place in God's economy and to act accordingly. Forming and maintaining this common perspective will result in a united body capable of manifesting a politics worthy of those "in Christ."[20]

Undertaking such a task, the pastor soon discovers that he or she is not surrounded by a massive number of individuals with unending needs to be fulfilled. Instead, the pastor discovers sisters and brothers, the saints, in the body of Christ, each uniquely gifted to make the life of the church manifest in an unbelieving world. The pastor's task is to help the congregation to discern the precise local embodiment of its witness as the church. The pastor may then help the congregation persevere in

---

[18]Stanley Hauerwas and William H. Willimon, *Resident Aliens: A Provocative Christian Assessment of Culture and Ministry for People Who Know That Something Is Wrong* (Nashville: Abingdon, 1989), pp. 139-40.
[19]Ibid., p. 140.
[20]Fowl, *Philippians,* p. 86.

this witness so that its Christian peculiarity might be evident to those who encounter its life. This task is not depleting but empowering.

The homiletical approach of turning, as described in chapters three and four, will assist the formation of the church as a peculiar people as the Holy Spirit works within the Word proclaimed. Yet words alone will not provide a sufficient rhetoric to persuade or embody this call to be an alternative community of Christ. For it to maintain its credibility and witness, the sermon itself must be embedded in a wider set of pastoral and congregational practices. Given how deeply we have been shaped by the expressive individualism of American culture, we must see ourselves in a completely new manner. This will take all the resources of a congregation and all the pastoral skills that a pastor may muster. Regarding this, Fowl writes:

> If we are to unlearn our commitments to individualism and to begin to embody the sort of common life to which Paul and the Philippians call us, we must come to share with them the sense of being caught up into the movement of God's economy of salvation. At its roots the friendship, and thus, the accountability, between Paul and the Philippians comes from their conviction that they have been made fellow participants in God's gracious redemption of the world in Christ. Unless and until we can see our lives as having been incorporated into that larger drama of redemption, we will never be able to see the necessity for the sort of ecclesial common life Paul urges on the Philippians.[21]

This common life of friendship and accountability in the church provides the context for a long and powerful life in the pastorate and a reason, week after week, to redirect the people of God into a faithful performance of God's story.

Congregational Life as the Rhetorical Embodiment of the Story

Words are always embedded in social contexts and practices. These contexts not only determine and clarify meaning, they also provide the moral credibility and power that words carry. To weave the story of God we must not only reiterate the biblical narrative's difference from the stories of the world, the narrative must be embedded in certain practices of

---

[21]Ibid., p. 88.

a congregation—and its pastor—for it to continue to form a congregation into a peculiar people as a faithful witness of God's present and coming reign.

Preaching is one practice that God has given the church to maintain the faithfulness of its witness. If the church were to lose preaching as a vital Christian practice—and there have been times within the history of the church when it has—the witness of the church suffers profoundly. Yet preaching alone will not insure the faithfulness of the church's witness. When preaching becomes separated from the biblical narrative, even if the biblical text survives, it will serve a community other than the church. Other ecclesial practices must provide the context for preaching, even as preaching provides a verbal context for other ecclesial practices. Together, a rhetoric of preaching that accepts a tragic moment for the reformation of a congregation may gain its specific Christian persuasive force when placed within a rhetorical context of specific congregational practices. I would like to suggest three particular congregational practices that may guide preaching so that it remains within the biblical narrative.

The Lord's Supper. The most important ecclesial practice that provides a rhetorical context for the renarrating of a congregation's life is the Lord's Supper. The Lord's Supper, of course, is firmly encoded in the biblical text and has always, until recent centuries, been at the center of all Christian worship. This unique practice of the church enacts, in dramatic form, the central event of the biblical narrative, the death, resurrection and return of Jesus. The Lord's Supper forms the church as a unique, peculiar people—the body of Christ. Only faithful living within the biblical narrative can render intelligible the Christian practice of gathering at the Table to eat the body and drink the blood of Jesus. As we read in the Gospel of John, Jesus said, "I tell you the truth, unless you eat the flesh of the Son of Man and drink his blood, you have no life in you" (Jn 6:53).[22] The Lord's Supper maintains coherence as a congregational practice only when practiced within the biblical narrative.

The Lord's Supper places a congregation's life into a particular narra-

---

[22]Of course, we should note as well that "from this time many of his disciples turned back and no longer followed him" (Jn 6:66).

tive structure as the reason for their existence. In the gift of the body of Christ given in the Lord's Supper, God calls forth a specific congregation as the present body of Christ, living between Christ's passion and the eschatological renewal of all creation, when the saints will be gathered together by God in the kingdom come in its fullness.

The faithful performance of the Supper prepares and empowers a congregation to embrace its unique Christian mission. William Cavanaugh says:

> The task of the church in the temporal order is to embody what Christ has already accomplished in history by re-membering his broken and victorious body. Christ's victory is already won, and the Kingdom is to have transformative effects on Christian practice in history. The task of the church is to live as if this is the case, until Christ comes again and fully consummates his reign.[23]

The Lord's Supper both creates and demands the biblical narrative, even as it creates and demands the church as a peculiar people. The Eucharist provides a rhetorical basis for weaving a congregation and individuals within the congregation into God's story.

Positively, the practice of the Lord's Supper grants the pastor great authority to call a congregation into the biblical narrative. After all, calling the church to "do this in remembrance" was not the pastor's idea, but Jesus'! The fact that the Scriptures call for believers to partake of the body and the blood of Jesus opens up pastoral venues for congregational formation and evangelization to those outside the faith, homiletically and otherwise. To place the believer within the biblical narrative as a "communicant" in Christian education, Bible study, and especially baptismal preparation can help laity understand how God has gathered them into a different story, God's story, from that which is being lived out by the world.

The fact that the Christian life and church's witness flows out of the participation in the Supper grants opportunities for congregational reflection on the nature of the Christian life and witness in the world. By

---

[23]William T. Cavanaugh, "The City: Beyond Secular Parodies," in *Radical Orthodoxy: A New Theology*, ed. John Milbank, Catherine Pickstock and Graham Ward (London: Routledge, 1999), p. 185.

practicing the Lord's Supper, the church must continually justify this practice within God's story, a justification that itself demands theological, moral and political re-formation.

The theological guidance provided by the practice of the Lord's Supper is not merely for the laity. The Supper also gives theological guidance for pastor's crafting of a sermon. Whether or not the Supper is practiced weekly, preaching can always be both eucharistic and evangelical in the fullest sense of both terms by asking a simple question: Could this sermon be followed coherently by an invitation to the Table to partake of the body and blood of Jesus? If it does not, if the Lord's Supper seems extraneous to the sermon or demands a shift in the direction of a service, the sermon most likely serves a community different from the church. It most likely has slipped into a therapeutic individualism, not the formation of the body of Christ in the world.

If the sermon can lead directly and smoothly to the Table (and if it can, then maybe it should!), the pastor can confidently proclaim God's Word with the hope that the Spirit can so work to re-form the congregation at its deepest convictional level to live within God's story as the body of Christ in the world. The practice of the Lord's Supper provides a rhetorical context for a homiletic that seeks the weaving of the congregation into the biblical narrative.

Negatively, a congregation that does not—or will not—regularly practice the Lord's Supper will have difficulty being woven into the biblical narrative. Quite simply, there is no reason why the church should be drawn to remember the body and blood of Christ if the church itself is insignificant except as a service organization to meet individual therapeutic needs. Such a congregation is already tragic. Its members will exercise with extreme difficulty Christian discernment. The Spirit's work to bring forth Christian virtues will be severely inhibited and the witness of the saints within it will be muted. To highlight such a tragedy through a rhetoric of difference that is spoken truthfully and compassionately represents hope for the Christian witness of such a congregation.

Forgiveness. All other Christian practices that provide a rhetorical context for the homiletical weaving of God's story are already embedded within the practice of the Lord's Supper. For instance, the Lord's Supper both presupposes the forgiveness of the believer and the believer's forgiveness—that is, the forgiveness of sins that arises from the death and resurrection of Christ and the Christian's forgiveness of others in order to be gathered to the Table. Thus Christian forgiveness provides a second practice that forms a favorable rhetorical context for weaving a congregation into the biblical narrative.

Christian forgiveness is a uniquely Christian practice. Anchored in the body of Christ, the crucified, sacramental and ecclesial body of Christ, Christian forgiveness has a distinctive nature because it has a distinctive basis and distinctive end. Christian forgiveness does not begin with the individual but with God's forgiveness of the individual through the death and resurrection of Christ in his or her incorporation into the people of God. The Gospels are very clear, however, that receiving forgiveness from God must lead to the forgiveness of others. Christians pray for the forgiveness of their trespasses as they forgive those who trespass against them.

Christian forgiveness is not an end unto itself. Being forgiven, Christians forgive because forgiveness provides space for reconciliation to take place. Forgiveness acknowledges wrongs and then moves beyond, not in forgetfulness but in a willingness to move into the future together with the one who has wronged. Yet even reconciliation is not an end in itself. The Christian practice of reconciliation points beyond itself so that the unity of the church might become visible so that the world may know the love of the triune God, and in knowing it might believe.

Being forgiven by God leads to the Christian practice of forgiveness, which leads to reconciliation, which leads to unity as the moral basis for evangelism. The Christian practice of forgiveness allows Christians to be reconciled by God at the Table of the Lord so that we might be made one and thus open the Table to others who, by faith, might come in the same divine forgiveness by which the saints already are gathered.

Christian forgiveness, therefore, differs from mere therapeutic forgiveness.[24] Christian forgiveness can participate in the same good for the forgiver while it looks far beyond the forgiver's own self-interests for fulfillment. Therapeutic forgiveness focuses on the deliverance that the self receives from its forgiveness of others. Without denying this deliverance

---

[24]See L. Gregory Jones, *Embodying Forgiveness: A Theological Analysis* (Grand Rapids: Eerdmans, 1995), esp. pp. 35-69.

of the self, Christian forgiveness is other directed rather than self-directed. The Christian end of forgiveness is reconciliation, especially for the reconciliation of brothers and sisters in Christ. It presupposes and demands the particularity of the biblical narrative, even as it lends credence to the truthfulness of this narrative through its communal embodiment.

Pastors know the importance of the practice of forgiveness within a congregation for the church's witness, especially when a congregation does not hide behind an imposed anonymity. In the complex life that makes up a congregation, the practice of forgiveness allows the unified mission of the congregation to take place unimpeded. The importance of forgiveness is seen especially when it is absent. When a husband and wife cannot forgive and be reconciled, it calls into question the difference between Christian marriage and marriages done at the local justice of the peace. When two members of a church board have a falling out without forgiveness, it changes the whole ability of the board to work together for the common good of the congregation and its witness. When a congregation's history is determined by rivalries between competing families for control of the church, the surrounding community watches as the church may undergo periods of growth, only to implode over and over again.

Caught at the center of the complex relationships of a congregation, the practice of forgiveness sustains the unity of a congregation, which is crucial for the rhetorical credibility of the pastor in weaving God's story homiletically. When a pastor becomes estranged from a congregation due to a failure to forgive or to seek and receive forgiveness, it becomes impossible to embrace a homiletical tragic moment to weave people into the biblical narrative. The call for the congregation to move into the biblical narrative will be heard as pastoral resentment or as a claim of clerical moral supremacy or self-righteousness. The congregation is left to take sides between the pastor and the members with whom the pastor is estranged. The gathering of the church in worship becomes a staging ground for a pitched battle rather than a way station for the pilgrim people of God. In this simple but profoundly real way the unity of the church suffers. As the unity of the church suffers, so does its witness. Who wants to be gathered into place of resentment as a context for worship? It is difficult to believe in the reconciling power of God in Jesus

Christ when the body of Christ in the world is fractured and antagonistic.

That is not to say that the pastor becomes a sacrificial whipping post for the sinful outbursts of those shaped by the fallenness of the world. Christian forgiveness presupposes truthfulness. Forgiveness as defined by the biblical narrative must acknowledge the wrong done. Yet the wrong done is not the last word for Christians, nor is it a word that calls for retaliation. Christian forgiveness seeks to overcome a wrong through mercy and reconciliation, and thereby becomes an embodied sign of the nature of God. Even if the offer of forgiveness is not accepted, the offering of mercy remains a sign of God's love in Jesus, a token of the kingdom that will come in its fullness.

Embedded within a forgiven, forgiving and reconciled and reconciling people, the pastor's practice of forgiveness sets a rhetorical context whereby a tragic homiletic can be freely offered. The tragic is overcome not by denial, forgetfulness or retaliation, but by fully divine *and* fully human mercy, the mercy of Jesus Christ. Tragedy, even as experienced, is real; yet the tragic is no longer the last word. As overcome in forgiveness, the tragic moment opens a new possibility for life within God's people that only can exist on the other side of the tragic. Despair becomes replaced by hope; a self-directed past opens into a divine vocation amid a people in the future. A congregational embodiment of the practice of forgiveness takes away the threat, not the force, of the tragic moment. It allows others to hear with openness rather than resistance; those who have ears will be able to hear. In hearing, then, the Spirit may enfold individuals into the biblical narrative as part of the people of God.

Sharing and hospitality. A third practice provides a positive rhetorical context for renarrating human life into the biblical narrative—the practice of sharing of material goods with believers and hospitality toward strangers. The Lord's Supper again encloses this practice of shared goods and hospitality. In the Lord's Supper a congregation, by faith, partakes in Christ's body and blood, and become a community of shared goods—literally, the shared good of the cup and the bread. What the church performs at the Table, the Scriptures enjoin as normative for the practice of the church outside of worship. In Romans, Paul says, "Share with God's people ["the saints"] who are in need. Practice hospitality" (Rom 12:13). Lest we think that this exhortation is a Pauline idiosyncrasy, in Hebrews the same order appears in different words: "Keep on loving each other as brothers. Do not forget to entertain strangers, for by so doing some people have entertained angels without knowing it" (Heb 13:1-2). First John also states strongly:

> If anyone has material possessions and sees his brother in need but has no pity on him, how can the love of God be in him? Dear children, let us not love with words or tongue but with actions and in truth. This then is how we know that we belong to the truth, and how we set our hearts at rest in this presence. (1 Jn 3:17-19)

Material goods are for the common good of the congregation and are used as a witness through hospitality to those outside the body.

The practice of material sharing and hospitality is not an isolated moral duty enjoined merely by divine fiat but arises out of and is supported by the biblical narrative. Those who live within this narrative participate in practices appropriate to their community. Israel, for example, left the gleanings of their fields for Israel's poor and for the sojourners in the land. The Jubilee sought to restore the land to the whole people of God. The prophets repeatedly called Israel to care for the orphan and the widow in the cities of Israel, as they too were part of the elect. Divine election demands a sharing of communal resources from those who have to those who need.

The biblical narrative refocuses the practice of sharing economic resources to needy brothers and sisters within the life of the church. The church, the elect in Jesus Christ, continues Israel's practice of using its material resources for the common good. Election into the household of God brings special economic relationships within the church that operate as a harmonious community rather than a competitive marketplace.

Yet the material resources of a congregation are not gathered merely for the sustenance of the baptized. The church also practices hospitality to strangers. Strangers come to a congregation not as a threat but as a gift, reminding Christians that they themselves were once strangers to God. Hospitality makes sure that a congregation does not curve in on itself. Even as the God they serve, they open themselves individually and corporately to the neighbor met along the road, even one beaten and bloody, in generosity and mercy. The economic resources shared in hospitality declare to the world the undeserved grace of God in a concrete, embodied manner.

The practice of sharing economic goods among believers and being hospitable to strangers is the context for understanding the church's commitment to the poor, the sick and the jailed—those whom society relegates to its margins. Placed within the context of shared communal goods and hospitality, the ministry to the poor is saved from a liberal paternalism. The poor are not a problem to be solved outside the church. The baptized poor *are* the church with whom God calls all believers into solidarity and care; the unbaptized poor are strangers to whom the church practices hospitality. The poor and the marginalized come as a gift, enabling the church to witness that God's abundant grace overcomes economic barriers that the society constructs to protect the self-interest of others.

Through mutual care and hospitality, the church absorbs economic barriers into its common life. These class barriers often have ethnic, linguistic and national dimensions. In the practice of sharing and hospitality, the church witnesses to the eschatological in-gathering of all humanity into God's present but not-yet-fully consummated kingdom. In its economic practices the church gives a glimpse of the day when every knee shall bow and every tongue confess that Jesus Christ is Lord, to the glory of God the Father.

The poor of the church receive from the bounty of the whole. Hospitality to strangers is not a social welfare system that seeks to give the poor the same consumer rights as the wealthy. Nor is it a selfless act of benevolence from an individual who has received God's blessing. Mutual care and hospitality again arise out of the nature of the church drawn together at the Lord's Supper:

> The Eucharist aims to build the body of Christ, which is not simply centripetal: we are united not just to God, as to the center, but to one another. This is no liberal body, in which the center seeks to maintain the independence of individuals from each other, nor a fascist body, which seeks to bind individuals to each other through the center. Christ is indeed the Head of the Body, but the members do not relate to one another through the Head alone, for Christ himself is found not only in the center but at the margins of the Body, radically identified with the "least of my brothers

and sisters" . . . with whom all the members suffer and rejoice together.
. . . Christ is the center of the eucharistic community, but in the economy
of the Body of Christ, gift, giver, and recipient are constantly assimilated,
one to another, such that Christ is what we receive, He who gives it, and
'the least' who receives the gift, and we are assimilated to Christ in all
three terms.[25]

The sharing of goods in the church and hospitality for strangers is a part
and parcel of the church itself.

Such practice runs counter to the dominant economic practices of the
North American society. Economic resources are, first, about individual
and family consumption, according to personal values and future prosperity. Corporately, economics is about the firm's competitive position
in the marketplace. It is impossible to long maintain the practices of
shared goods and hospitality when such narratives define the church. As
a result the church's witness is eroded over time when it accommodates
such economics.

When a consumerist story determines the financial practices of the
church, the church's material goods, the offerings of its members, become given as either payment for the services that the church provides
or as an investment for future divine or material blessings. In either case,
personal and institutional self-interests become determinative. It becomes increasingly difficult to maintain financial harmony within the
congregation.

Consumerist economics undercut the distinct moral nature of the
church. When the economics of personal interest rather than shared
goods defines the church's redistribution of its wealth, the church's witness is undermined. Take, for instance, the financial support given to
most pastors by congregations. Within the economic system of the society, the pastor gets paid for his or her job (salaried, of course, so that
the church will not have to pay overtime!) according to the highest possible salary that the pastor can negotiate. The governing board must protect the interests of the contributors by paying the least possible to ensure the type of service they want from the pastor.

A whole understanding of a common good that enables the congre-

---

[25]Cavanaugh, "City: Beyond Secular Parodies," p. 196.

gation to free the pastor from financial pressures so that he or she might engage in the work of the ministry is lost. Rather than witnessing to the mutuality of goods by the care and provision of the pastor, the church takes on the nature of the competing economic interests of the contributors and the pastor. Because it is built on a system that presupposes and encourages economic conflict, conflict usually will emerge, with either the pastor or the congregation losing in the process. In both cases the witness of the church as a whole suffers in its relationships with those outside it. Deep resentments (within the congregation or the pastor) arise that quickly become communicated to those outside the congregation.

When the society's economic narrative defines the church's economics, resources are inevitably used to improve the church's position in the marketplace, usually by showing increased status in property and by providing expanded services to the middle and upper-middle class. This is no accident. If the church is a service firm, it must recruit more members with personal economic resources to pay for the services provided. Hopefully increased services produce increased surplus revenue. The profit margin can then be used to subsidize noncontributors, both within and outside the congregation. Even if not intentionally, the poor are structurally excluded from the services of the church, except as recipients of special, periodic benevolence. Hospitality is practiced, but to a select demographic group rather than the stranger found on the road. Economic class becomes more determinative than baptism; nationality and ethnicity overcome being made one in Christ in baptism and at the Table.

Ultimately the church's witness becomes completely assimilated into the society. With no difference between the church and the society, it is no longer beneficial to self-interests to contribute in volunteer hours or finances. It becomes harder and harder for the ecclesial firm to generate income, and thus harder and harder to sustain its services. Ministries implode, and the church begins a painful cycle of decline unless reinvigorated by an energetic, gifted pastor/entrepreneur.

The congregational practice of caring for the needs of the saints and showing hospitality to strangers provides a positive rhetorical context for moving people through a tragic homiletical moment and into God's story as part of the peculiar people. First, mutual care and hospitality show the tragic moment to be just that—a moment. Material sharing produces a vitality of common life that highlights the long-term tragedy of life lived to fulfill its own self-interests outside the people of God. Mutual support provides a much richer life than self-imposed isolation and self-interest. Thanksgiving arises out of participating in a mutuality of life. Thanksgiving transforms the context of the gathering of the saints into the type of community described in Philippians rather than in *Habits of the Heart*. The narratives of individual fulfillment become morally overwhelmed when confronted with a living, breathing people who dwell in community. Their very existence proves that life can indeed be different!

Second, in accepting the stranger and embracing the poor as a gift—even those who are ungrateful—the moral vision of a congregation shifts. Bodily interaction across economic, ethnic, national and linguistic lines moves past stereotyping and draws people into accountability as members of the one body of Christ. People cease to become broad demographic statistics. In the midst of the church community, the individuality of each person becomes most evident. Individuality not only brings specific gifts to the congregation but also helps empower the church to address the complex particularity of individual needs. Finally, interaction with the poor of the church and the strangers forces a congregation to gather for specifically Christian purposes. The only reason for the particular group that God gathers in worship has to come from its center, Jesus Christ, rather than demographic categories provided by Madison Avenue.

The pastor's role in caring for the needs of the saints and hospitality to strangers must occur within a wider congregational practice. Unless a broader congregational practice is at work, the pastor will quickly fall into the therapeutic trap of trying to meet all needs of the congregation. The pastor does not embody the whole church but plays a particular role within the larger body. Yet the pastor cannot completely delegate care for the poor, visitation of the sick and those in prison, and hospitality for the stranger to the laity. The pastor must be specially aligned with the sick, the poor and the stranger, having personal contact with them and being their advocate. This is especially true for a tragic homiletic moment to be credible for the congregation and the world.

This advice runs counter to that of many current pastoral leadership experts. Leadership material that advises the pastor to seek out the most powerful and influential (and thereby, often the wealthiest) individuals within a church has replaced the ordination commission to care for the poor, the sick, and the disenfranchised. Yet the biblical narrative calls forth a community in which the poor are blessed because the kingdom of God is theirs. Inevitably, those with whom the pastor spends the bulk of his or her time shapes his or her moral perspective. By visiting with the poor, the pastor not only steers clear of various patronage struggles of the influential within a congregation but also ensures that all are enfolded in pastoral care. The whole congregation, rich and poor alike, may hear the pastor's preaching as a call to participation in the people of God based on Christ's atoning death for all rather than a power play for the patronage of a few influential members.

These three congregational practices—the Lord's Supper, forgiveness and reconciliation, and caring for the needs of the saints and hospitality offered to strangers—shift the rhetorical context of preaching from the categories of the wider society to the categories appropriate for the church as a peculiar people. Such a congregation's witness becomes apparent in their Christian peculiarity. These practices form a congregational context for preaching that makes evident that the preacher is not calling people into abstract concepts but into a concrete community that lives within the biblical narrative. This living, breathing community permits the tragic moment in preaching to be experienced as a call to something truer and more life-empowering than narratives of individual and social upward mobility. The pastor who ministers as one enfolded within the narrative becomes an embodied witness to the narrative shift proclaimed from the pulpit. The congregational context makes apparent that a fullness of life as part of the pilgrim people of God, "the life that is truly life" (1 Tim 6:19), lies on the other side of the tragic moment. The congregation becomes the only apologetic needed. No longer does the biblical text need to be translated into individual lives; individuals now have a reason to be translated into God's story.

The Demands of a Tragic Homiletical Rhetoric

Congregational practices that arise from living within God's story provide a rhetorical context in which the renarrating of life can take place. Yet moving a congregation into this narrative homiletically is not without its dangers. Preaching to form a peculiar people will bring forth resistance both within and outside a congregation until conversion takes place. Conversion of a congregation to living within the biblical narrative is one of the greatest hopes, privileges and adventures of the contemporary pastorate. Given the positive rhetorical context of congregational and pastoral practices, there are nonetheless special homiletical traps the pastor needs to avoid to weave God's story faithfully for a congregation. I would like to briefly mention two.

First, contextually sensitive, rhetorical excellence is required. Faithful content is no excuse for poor presentation. Hearing a sermon that seeks to form the church into a contrast society places high demands on a congregation in the first place. The North American culture has formed church members to expect sermons to lead immediately to practical therapeutic advice. Members undoubtedly will struggle just to hear. Word meanings shift according to the underlying narratives that confer sense on them. Confusion can and often will result, even among the best-intentioned listeners. The more difficult the task of communication, the less room there is for poor communication skills. We must seek to keep the scandal of the gospel in the right place—in the gospel, not in poor rhetorical skills, lack of creativity or inadequate preparation.

The homiletic that I advocate should not reduce preaching to an elitist "talking manuscript" approach. Engagement with the congregation is necessary and good. The sermons of Augustine, transcribed by scribes as he actually preached, evidence a congregation that cheered and even booed Augustine while he spoke. Preaching cannot deny the particular embodied, historical existence of a congregation, not if it seeks to shape that existence into the particularity that is the church in its local manifestation. Rhetorical engagement with the congregation is necessary, but not an end unto itself. Rhetorical engagement must serve the difference found in the gospel, not naming what is already present in the individual's experience. Rhetorical skill must effectively call people into the body of Christ through faith.

The pastor should listen carefully to feedback, positive and negative. The most likely critique will be, "I'm not being fed" or "The sermons are not meeting my needs." Yet some criticism may reflect problems in delivery that distract from the renarration taking place. Preaching to form a faithful, alternative people is more demanding than usual, both on the preacher and those listening. Close attention to the feedback of the people, even those who resist taking part in God's story, can help the rhetorical shaping of the sermon for the particular context of the congregation.

Second, the pastor cannot use the tragic moment to beat up a congregation. Truthfulness is required in preaching; indeed, we must occasionally go "from preachin' to meddlin' " lest the proclamation of the gospel lose its concreteness. We must "speak the truth in love," even to the point of acknowledging and identifying with the suffering of the people in the midst of a narrative shift.

A pastor preached a sermon titled "Rags-to-Riches Faith to the Riches-to-Rags Jesus." When the sanctuary had emptied after the service, a member of the congregation approached. With tears welling up, the member said, "You just said that all I've ever believed in is wrong." The pastor said, "I know," and the two openly wept together in the empty sanctuary. If we are engaged in the practices of the biblical narrative so that the virtues of the narrative are emerging within our own character, preaching into and through the tragic moment must be seen as part of our own self-emptying in obedience, not as a bully's stick to bludgeon a wayward congregation.

It is important to realize that preaching does not transform people; the Holy Spirit does. If the congregation consistently has the rug pulled out from under them merely to have the rug pulled out, they will become calloused and unable to hear the truthfulness of the final movements of the sermon. We must reassure the congregation that repentance is good; it points toward the concrete communal formation and practices that are happening and will happen within a congregation's life. The gospel is ultimately a comedy. We cannot get so wrapped up in the consistent calling for a deep narrative reworking of human lives that the glorious end of the gospel gets lost. Pastoral wisdom is constantly required, a wisdom that arises out of the our involvement in the lives of those within the congregation.

Preaching to form the church as a peculiar people brings dangers to the pastor. It calls for the best rhetorical skills. Perhaps more importantly, it calls for the preacher, while preaching, to manifest the Christian virtues of faith, hope and love. It calls for the pastor to not only proclaim the alternative story of God—who created all there is from nothing, called Israel into existence, sent the Son to graft Gentiles into God's elect, and ultimately will restore all creation to its original goodness—it also calls for the pastor to live within this narrative as it is proclaimed in the power of the Spirit for the upbuilding of the body for faithful witness in the world.

Conclusion

This chapter has addressed the congregational discomfort that can come by renarrating people lives into God's story and suggested ways of overcoming the discomfort. The task seems so daunting because of the acceptance of the therapeutic that defines and makes so difficult pastoral ministry today. There is a therapeutic result from the gospel, but we do not discover it within the interior, private life of autonomous individuals but in the concrete, embodied existence of the people of God. Only by living within a peculiar people may the pastor escape the devastating sinfulness that arises from the therapeutic demands placed on the pastor by an unbelieving North American society.

Overcoming the therapeutic expectations on the pastor demands alternative practices that establish a context for the proclamation and reception of sermons. A set of three practices play a particularly important re-formation of a congregation: (1) the Lord's Supper, (2) forgiveness, reconciliation and congregational unity, and (3) caring for the needs of the saints and showing hospitality to strangers. These practices must be embedded in the biblical narrative to maintain their coherence as Christian practices, but they also call forth a people who live within the biblical narrative. Together, they provide an apologetic for moving into and through a tragic homiletical moment. They visibly show that the tragic moment in a sermon is not to be feared or resisted; it is not the last word. We can accept the untruth of previous narratives in order to live by the true narrative of the Scriptures. This apology is not found in an abstract idea or individual experience, or in the objective historicity of the Bible, but in the concrete existence of a people, sanctified by the Spirit for faithful witness to God.

Pastoring a congregation to live within the Christian Scriptures, rather than merely assent to them, is a tremendous adventure. It only makes sense if we genuinely believe that God has raised Christ from the grave and that God has called the church to witness to this resurrection by its very life in preparation for the time when the kingdom of God will be on earth as it is in heaven. Neither triviality nor boredom will ever characterize such a life, though suffering may—and at times, most certainly will—ensue. The key is to suffer for the right reasons—for the kingdom of God and its righteousness rather than our own inadequacies or sinfulness. In this, however, we are surrounded by a cloud of witnesses who have gone before us, including Jesus, the author and perfector of our faith. With such confidence, God calls us forward.

CONCLUSION

Two fundamentally different approaches to the mission of the church have arisen in North America in recent years. One approach looks first to the world to determine the agenda for the church. The givenness of the world allows the church to refashion its inner resources and spiritual life to meet more effectively the world's needs as determined by the present age. The other approach looks first to the inner resources and spiritual life of the church and then to the world. The church learns to engage the world from within its own inner life so that its witness might call the church and the world to a profound conversion arising out of the faith given to the saints through the ages.

These two different approaches can overlap in practice, depending on particular traditions and particular cultural and social contexts. Both agree that we should not isolate the church from the world, and that the church should not abandon its own resources and traditions. The two understandings can even approach each other in specific areas according to the relative weight put on the church's inner resources or on the contemporary setting. Yet even as these approaches can and do approach each other in practice, a deep underlying conceptual fault nonetheless remains.[1]

If we look closely, we can see that this difference runs throughout North American Christianity in its evangelical, mainline Protestant and Roman Catholic manifestations. Evangelicals tend to dispute this differ-

---

[1]I have adapted these categories from an essay by George Lindbeck on contemporary ecumenism. See George Lindbeck, "Ecumenisms in Conflict: Where Does Hauerwas Stand?" in *God, Truth, and Witness: Engaging Stanley Hauerwas*, ed. L. Gregory Jones, Reinhard Hütter and C. Roslee Velloso Ewell (Grand Rapids: Brazos, 2005), pp. 212-28.

ence in their assessment of the church growth movement, its application and underlying theological convictions.[2] Mainline Protestants dispute the issue in terms of liberationist or confessional agendas, the dialogue between liberal or postliberal theological convictions. Within Roman Catholicism, we experience this difference in disputes between those seeking accommodation and influence within their contemporary national environment[3] versus those in the new religious movements such as Communion and Liberation who seek a type of catholicity that transcends the locality of time and space in a communion of the saints under the bishop of Rome.[4]

This book has entered this ongoing dispute. I have argued that preaching must first and foremost call people into the inner life of the church in Christ to guide congregations to witness to the world, to call the world and individuals within it to God in and through Christ by the power of the Holy Spirit. Allowing North American culture, history, presuppositions and institutions to form the fundamental categories of our preaching is like selling the farm before putting it on the market.

In many ways the church has always functioned within the tension between its inner resources and its immediate environment for its mission. To conclude this book, I would like to look at a master theologian and preacher who wrote the first "preaching manual" in the history of the church—Augustine, bishop of Hippo. Augustine did the bulk of his theological work as a pastor. In his letters we even find complaints con-

---

[2]See, i.e., the work of George Barna (*The Habits of Highly Effective Churches: Being Strategic in Your God Given Ministry* [Ventura, Calif.: Regal Books, 1999]; *A Step-by-Step Guide to Church Marketing: Breaking Ground for Harvest* [Ventura, Calif.: Regal Books, 1992]) versus that of David F. Wells in his works, *No Place for Truth, or Whatever Happened to Evangelical Theology* (Grand Rapids: Eerdmans, 1993); *God in the Wasteland: The Reality of Truth in a World of Fading Dreams* (Grand Rapids: Eerdmans, 1994); *Losing Our Virtue: Why the Church Must Recover Its Moral Vision* (Grand Rapids: Eerdmans, 1999); and *Above All Earthly Powers: Christ in a Postmodern World* (Grand Rapids: Eerdmans, 2005).

[3]From this perspective, Catholic liberals and neoconservatives, often at odds with each other, share much more in common in their ecclesiology than that by which they differ.

[4]One can see the fundamentally different perspectives in two post-Vatican II journals, *Concilium* and the *Communio;* in European Catholicism, we might analyze the difference as that between Hans Küng and Joseph Ratzinger; in the United States today, we might see this difference between Catholic neoconservatives such as Robert Novak, Richard John Neuhaus and George Weigel versus theologians such as David L. Schindler. See David L. Schindler *Heart of the World, Center of the Church: Communio Ecclesiology, Liberalism, and Liberation* (Grand Rapids: Eerdmans, 1996).

cerning the mundane busyness of overseeing the church that kept him from the intellectual and spiritual tasks that he preferred—complaints to which any contemporary pastor could add a hearty amen! In his preaching Augustine deeply engaged the rhetoric of his age, yet even as he did, he redirected the goal of preaching, much as I have argued, so that his congregation, and all Christian congregations, might find themselves as characters participating in God's redemption of the world through Christ and the church.

The Rhetoric of Preaching in *De Doctrina Christiana*

Rhetoric stood at the height of intellectual life in late antiquity, the world in which Augustine lived. Skill in rhetoric provided the means by which a young, brilliant man from North Africa might rise in status and honor within the late Western Roman Empire. With strong encouragement from his father, Augustine embarked on such a journey—and experienced considerable success. Augustine lived and moved and had his being in the competitive rhetorical context of late-fourth-century Roman society.

Yet God had other ideas for Augustine's rhetorical skills. Soon after he became bishop of Hippo in A.D. 396, Augustine began a work called *De Doctrina Christiana,* or *Teaching Christianity.*[5] His goal was twofold: to provide a guide for interpreting Scriptures "to discover what needs to be understood," and training preachers in "a way to put across to others what has been understood" (1.1). He quickly completed two books to guide readers on how to read the Scriptures. He began a third book to help Christian preachers understand the Scriptures. Yet other duties intervened. It was over thirty years later that he completed the third book; finally he undertook the second task in book 4—to instruct preachers how to speak when preaching what they understood in the Scriptures.

Book 4 presupposes a depth of immersion in classical rhetoric that few today possess. Yet the contemporary preacher may still read Augustine with profit. For those who would underplay the importance of rhetoric in preaching, Augustine notes that since knowledge exists to teach

---

[5]This text has usually been translated into English as "On Christian Doctrine." All quotes in this chapter are taken from *Teaching Christianity (De Doctrina Christiana),* The Works of Saint Augustine: A Translation for the 21st Century 1.11, ed. Edmund Hill (Hyde Park, N.Y.: New City Press, 1996). Italics from original.

persons to "speak well," "why should good men not study to acquire the art, so that it might fight for truth, if bad men can prostitute it to the winning of their vain and misguided cases in the service of iniquity and error?" (4.3). Augustine knew that rhetoric "carried with it social respect, prestige, power, authority. In this sense, Christianity could not ignore it; rather, it was an important instrument in establishing its own position within society."[6] Augustine taught that "those who can speak and discuss things wisely, even though they cannot do so eloquently, must now undertake the task . . . in such a way as to benefit their listeners" (4.7).

Augustine recognized that rhetoric is not an end in itself. Powerful rhetoric also represents a danger. He continues, "Beware . . . of those whose unwisdom has a flood of eloquence at its command, and all the more so, the more their audience takes pleasure in things it is profitless to hear, and assumes that because they hear them speaking fluently, they are so also speaking the truth" (4.7). Preaching must speak from within the Christian revelation, the inner resources of the faith granted by God the Father through the Son by the Holy Spirit in the Scriptures and manifested in the life of the church.

Precisely at this point Augustine rejected the underlying presupposition of his own Greco-Roman rhetorical training. Rhetoric had three functions in Augustine's day: to teach, to delight, and to persuade. Classical rhetoricians ordered persuasion as the highest good. Not for Augustine. Teaching the truth must always come first; delight and persuasion only find their proper places in relationship to teaching the truth as found in the gospel. "In sharp contrast to how rhetoric was popularly perceived, [Augustine] subordinates eloquence to truth, a desire to please to clarity and concern that one be understood."[7] The preacher seeks to delight the hearer, not "for its own sake, but in order that matters which are being usefully and properly talked about . . . might the more readily win that audience's assent and stick in its memory" (4.55).

The speaker must not use rhetoric as a means of self-advancement or for personal honor, but in service of the Word and the congregation

---

[6]Carol Harrison, "The Rhetoric of Scripture and Preaching: Classical Decadence or Christian Aesthetic?" in *Augustine and His Critics: Essays in Honour of Gerald Bonner*, ed. Robert Dodaro and George Lawless (London and New York: Routledge, 2000), p. 216.
[7]Ibid., p. 220.

whom God has entrusted to one's pastoral care. At the rhetorical base of preaching for Augustine is a "plain mode" of speech, a style appropriate to enhance understanding and clarity of truthfulness. Augustine recognized that "where stubborn hearts need to be swayed to obedience by the very grandeur of the style, unless the speaker is listened to with understanding and with pleasure, he cannot be listened to with compliance" (4.58).

Augustine advises preachers to adopt an appropriate rhetoric so that the congregation might understand the truthfulness of the sermon—its witness as the revelation of the Word of God. The goal of preaching finds itself in the truthfulness of the Word of God, that is Jesus Christ, in the wisest way possible in order to witness to the truth:

> What therefore does it mean to speak not only eloquently but also wisely, if not to provide words that are sufficient in the plain style, brilliant in the moderate, vehement and forceful in the grand manner, but still for saying true things that really need to be heard? But if anyone is unable to do both, let him say wisely what he does not say eloquently, rather than say eloquently what he says unwisely. (4.61)

Preaching is not sophistry; nor is it given merely for a short-term response. Augustine's wisdom remains evident today: the preacher "should prefer to please with the substance of what he says more than with the words he says it in; nor should he imagine that a thing is said better unless it is said more truly; and as a teacher his words should be serving him, not he his words" (4.61). The rhetoric of preaching points past the sermon and past the preacher to the Scriptures and the truth of the Word of God. The Scriptures provide the inner resources within which the preacher seeks to engraft the congregation through the wise use of rhetoric.

The True Interpretation of Scripture in Christian Preaching

Augustine subordinates rhetoric to truthfulness because he is thoroughly convinced of the innate rhetorical power and beauty of the truth as witnessed to in the Scriptures. This truth is found within the Scriptures itself. Augustine points us back to the final end of the Scriptures through preaching: "*the fulfillment and the end of the law* and of all the divine scriptures is *love* (Rom 13:8; 1 Tm 1:5)" (1.39), particularly love of God and love of neighbor. Augustine pulls no punches in his frankness: "If it seems to you that you have understood the divine scriptures, or any part of them, in such a way that by this understanding you do not build up this twin love of God and neighbor, then you have not yet understood them" (1.40).

Telling God's story is telling a story of God's love in Jesus Christ. To preach is to invite human beings to turn and participate in this God who is love:

> This is how God showed his love among us: He sent his one and only Son into the world that we might live through him. This is love: not that we loved God, but that he loved us and sent his Son as an atoning sacrifice for our sins. . . .
>
> God is love. Whoever lives in love lives in God, and God in him. (1 Jn 4:9-10, 16).

We cannot look to the society around us to find the source or definition of love. At best, we will end up with a twisted understanding of love. Christians find love at the very heart of the inner life and resources of the church as witnessed to in the Scriptures. We find love as the mystery of the triune God who is Father, Son and Holy Spirit, the eternal interrelationship of divine Persons that is love. Telling God's story must begin with this love that has been revealed to us in Jesus Christ. Preaching demands a call to faith in Jesus Christ, a faith that requires as its corollary the authority of the Scriptures. Augustine knew this well. He wrote that "faith will start tottering if the authority of scripture is undermined" (1.41).

Faith in Christ as called forth by the Spirit simultaneously calls believers to participate in the God who is love through participating in God's story in Scriptures. Augustine recognized that the whole structure of Christian formation and witness stands or falls with the vitality of this particular faith in Christ. Augustine saw that profound consequences arise for members and congregations if faith begins to fail. A type of "domino effect" begins to take place. If an individual or congregation begins losing faith in Christ, Augustine knew that their vitality of love will simultaneously slacken: "with faith tottering, charity itself also begins to sicken. . . . If you fall from faith, you are bound also to fall from charity" (1.41).

Unlike some church-cycle theorists today, Augustine thought that fluctuations in faith and love are not necessary for individuals or congregations. Through preaching the proper end of Scripture, telling God's story to elicit faith and love, "you ensure that you also hope to come eventually to what you love. And so we have these three things, for whose sake all knowledge and all prophecy are pressed into service, faith, hope, charity" (1.41). In so leading a congregation into the Scriptures, a preacher guides a congregation, and the individuals within it, to the depths of the inner life of the faith that is so necessary to the witness as a congregation—the life of love: "When you come to realize that *the end of the law is love, from a pure heart, and a good conscience, and faith without pretense* (1 Tm 1:5), you will relate all the understanding of the divine scriptures to these three, and so be able to approach the story of those books without the least anxiety" (1.44).

Augustine helps us understand why we must subordinate the rhetoric of preaching to the teaching of truth, that is, Jesus Christ. No rhetorical flourish can substitute for the truthfulness of the love that arises from the reception of divine love through faith in Jesus. The mystery of the Spirit's work in our puny, inadequate words is not one that can be predicted, engineered or controlled for effectiveness. The Spirit blows where it will. We often discover long after the fact how God has sanctified our words as God's own Word.

Augustine himself speaks of this mystery. He tells of a time when he was called to intervene in a "local civil war" in a place called Caesarea of Mauritania. He spoke "to the best of my ability in order to root out such a cruel and inveterate evil from their hearts and habits." Tears finally sprung forth from the crowd as he spoke; eight years later Augustine could report that the violence had never reawakened (4.53).

Augustine had engaged in a homiletic of repentance. Writing toward the end of his life, with the full experience of years of pastoring, he reflected back on his life of preaching, "There are many other experiences which have taught me that people have shown by their groans rather than their shouts, sometimes also by their tears, and finally by the change in their lives, what the grandeur of a wise man's speech has achieved in them" (4.53).

I have written this book to celebrate "the grandeur of a wise man's speech" in telling God's story. Calling human beings, believers and unbelievers, into the biblical text in repentance requires that we read the Scriptures in love of God and neighbor. Repentance bears no shame for Christians. Groans, even tears, can bear witness to the mercies of God granted us through the forgiveness already offered us in the death and resurrection of Jesus Christ. God has called preachers to participate in "the change in their lives" by calling people into the biblical story. Through faithful preaching, the Spirit forms a faithful people to witness to the love that is God in a world torn by sin and violence.

Index